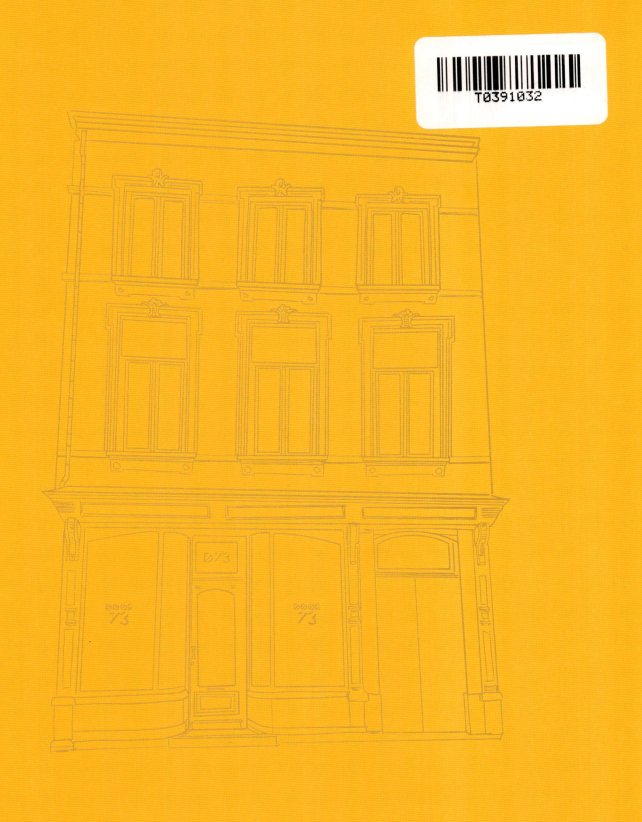

DOOR 73

the food vibes of
Eric Ivanidis and Marcelo Ballardin

Lannoo

WE EAGERLY TAKE IN EVERYTHING LIFE HAS TO OFFER. THAT'S WHY WE SELDOM SAY NO TO INTERESTING OPPORTUNITIES THAT COME OUR WAY.

The world revealed itself to me when I stepped onto a plane headed for the Netherlands. I was leaving with my wife Eleni for Cadzand, where Pure C, headed up by master chef Sergio Herman, had recently opened its doors. I felt irrevocably drawn to the restaurant and its dynamic surroundings, as if I instinctively felt I had to be there. Eleni became my tower of strength as she followed me and supported me in realising my big plan.

And then there was that first meeting with Marcelo, who became my trainee mentor and introduced me to local ingredients I had never even heard of. Our shared sense of humour and sunny, southern roots – Brazilian in his case, Greek in mine – led to an instant bond. And today, almost ten years after we left Pure C to establish his restaurant, OAK, in Ghent, he is still my guide – both personally and professionally.

Marcelo taught me to look ahead while keeping both feet firmly on the ground, no matter the situation. To stay rooted in my past. Greece is so much more than my country of birth; it is the place I draw my inspiration from. I am immensely grateful to my parents because they gave me all the freedom I needed and taught me the secrets of Greek cuisine with so much verve and flavour. On the one hand, this book is an ode to my mother, who, with her artisanal preparations of classics such as tarama, giouvetsi and moussaka, subconsciously drove me to become a family man and to pursue my career as a chef.

On the other hand, this book is a homage to the new family I have met here in Belgium. Marcelo, Dominik, their family, and the entire team at both OAK and DOOR73 took me in with warmth and love. Seeing how they maintain warm ties with my mother, sister, and cousins gives me great pleasure. The older I get, the more I feel it is important to share my life, vision and inspiration with my families. Especially when you have something valuable to pass on to others, as I do with my daughter. If I left tomorrow, DOOR73 should keep going. That's also the goal of this book.

I invite you, my guests and inquisitive readers, to embark on a journey of discovery guided by my personal story and 45 recipes, including 5 cocktails by Hannes Verniers. They tell part of the story of the life that I've led up until now and the experiences I've enjoyed. Finally, with DOOR73 and this book, I would like to bridge the different cultures, colours, and backgrounds that have inspired me thus far, each of which has contributed in its own way to the person I am today: a Greek, Flemish, Belgian cosmopolitan eager to explore the world.

Here's to plenty of cooking pleasure and culinary inspiration!

I hope to see you soon in our restaurant,

Eric Ivanidis

I believe that the question of whether to open a second restaurant arises with everyone after a successful first venture. And, to be perfectly honest with you, if it hadn't been for Eric, I probably never would have taken on this challenge. So, how did I make this decision?

It all comes down to our friendship. Eric has been an integral part of our business since OAK was established. Together with Dominik, he played a crucial role in OAK's development – from following up on recruitment to his pioneering work experimenting with private dining experiences. Eric stood by my side long before I had the privilege of welcoming our first guests at OAK.

He has been my faithful companion for over a decade. It has always been my goal to support him as much as possible. By the time the opportunity to open a second restaurant presented itself, Eric was thoroughly fed up with working beside me as a sous chef at OAK. It won't surprise you to know that conflicts arose more and more frequently in our kitchen. Nick Polak can testify to our epic discussions, which sometimes resembled fights more than anything else, as if an elder brother had taken up the gauntlet against his younger sibling.

I'm sharing these intimate details to highlight how my relationship with Eric is much more than just a superficial bond. We are more intimately connected than most other fellow chefs. I know his family, and he knows mine. I've been closely involved with his professional development, and I'm convinced beyond any doubt that he and his team currently embody the best culinary concept this country has to offer.

With DOOR73, Eric has succeeded in creating his own identity, and it fills me with pride to see how I've been able to contribute to this evolution. But his biggest achievement so far is becoming a father. So, I feel incredibly privileged to be a godfather to his daughter, Athina.

I share these personal stories to give you a glimpse into my unique bond with Eric, a relationship that goes much deeper than you would initially suspect.
Enjoy this book and our chemistry,

Marcelo Ballardin

OUR STORY

This book is our story. About how we are alike and yet make entirely different choices. Rooted in the family bonds we've chosen. This story would not be complete without Eric's Greek roots and my Brazilian origins. How we as outsiders have managed to build something new, far away from home. That his journey would take him from Crete, after a brief stop in the Netherlands, to the heart of Ghent to help me realise my dream of opening a restaurant. And also how Ghent welcomed him with open arms and spurred his decision to spread his wings here. DOOR73 is a melting pot of the cultures and cuisines that inspire him, seasoned with the culinary traditions from his homeland. In addition to becoming an entrepreneur, Eric became a different person through interaction with his surroundings, his team, and his family. And that is something that deserves respect.

21 **ABOUT US: FROM FRIENDS TO BUSINESS PARTNERS**

37 **ERIC'S GENEROUS GREEK ROOTS**

81 **BROTHERS IN CRIME**

107 **FROM PICTURESQUE ZEELAND TO BUSTLING GHENT**

131 **HITTING THE ROAD WITH A BACKPACK FULL OF INSPIRATION**

163 **HANNES' SOFT TOUCH**

RECIPE INDEX

COCKTAILS
- **22** Whisky sour
- **24** The blue beast
- **26** Not a ****** mule
- **28** Liqueur d'amour
- **30** Pineapple punch

STARTERS
- **40** Red beetroot tzatziki
- **44** Brioche with chicken mousse
- **50** Kalitsounia pasty
- **52** Grilled corn on the cob with tomato butter and Parmesan
- **54** Holstein tonnato
- **58** Chicken wings with barbecue sauce and aioli
- **60** Tiradito de Pescado
- **62** Tarama with sumac and chive oil
- **64** Ricotta with dried date tomatoes and caper leaf
- **66** Soft-shell crab tempura with wasabi mayonnaise
- **70** Pan de cristal with fried sardines
- **76** Fried artichokes
- **78** Shellfish à la Taiwan

COMFORT
- **82** Moussaka
- **86** Braised lamb shanks
- **90** Barbecued spring chicken
- **92** Aubergine alla parmigiana
- **94** Fish and chips with tarama
- **96** Grandma's meatloaf with mashed potatoes
- **100** Ossobuco giouvetsi
- **102** Seafood with tomato sauce

TRUST
- **112** Tomato burrata with muhammara
- **114** Fish pie
- **116** Green asparagus with crusty sourdough bread and spicy tomato sauce
- **118** Butter beans with sambal
- **122** Young cauliflower with tahini dressing, salsa, miso and dukkha
- **126** Grilled sea bass with caper dressing and parsley oil
- **128** Poached cod in red curry sauce

DISCOVERY
- **136** Chipotle portobello
- **138** Chicken tikka masala kataifi
- **142** Brazilian curry with gambero rosso and pimenta-de-bode chilli
- **144** Duck confit
- **146** Tomato salad with feta and oregano oil
- **148** Short ribs with cashews and barbecue sauce
- **153** North Sea crab with bahārāt, kritharaki and XO sauce
- **158** Hamachi kama with grilled kimchi
- **160** Mackerel with sambal and soy dressing

DESSERTS
- **168** Lemon kataifi with ras-el-hanout and buttermilk ice cream
- **172** Raspberry sundae with yuzu and yoghurt
- **176** Crème brûlée with rum and brioche
- **180** Donuts with vanilla ice cream and pistachio halva
- **184** Apple pie with mastiha ice cream

ABOUT US:
FROM FRIENDS TO BUSINESS PARTNERS

M   Few people realise that Eric and I are also close on a personal level. I am godfather to Eric's daughter, Athina. I always make time for her; we go for walks or grab a bite to eat somewhere, and I listen in admiration to her first words. I view the business that I run with my partner Dominik as a close-knit family. To be honest, our intention was never to run multiple restaurants but, because of Eric's talent and our close relationship with him, that's how things turned out. Eric and I maintain that personal connection with our own teams. For instance, we have certain rituals that we stick to. Just before our Christmas leave, Eric always makes a delicious moussaka, and I prepare a lasagne based on my father's recipe. After consuming these calorie bombs, we automatically roll into the holiday spirit. It is essential to make time for your team. We can only grow as chefs if our foundations are solid. Without their hands, hearts, and minds, there would be no restaurant. It's that simple. Respect for your team shouldn't only be expressed through a salary; it's often the small things that make a difference. Eating together and taking time to confer with each other. Bringing a bottle of wine for your sommelier when you have tasted something unique at a wine tasting. Getting your sous-chefs involved when cooking abroad. Organising a trip to the region where one of your producers is located. Only by inspiring your team will you be able to grow together. I always try to keep this long-term vision in the front of my mind.

E   Marcelo and I are good friends as well as professional partners. We encourage each other to bring out the best in ourselves. We share a particular mindset and drive; giving up is not in our vocabulary. But it doesn't end there. We strive to provide our guests with a good time that will hopefully inspire fond memories. People used to see DOOR73 as OAK's little brother, but today, my restaurant has its own identity with a family of its own, and that true of both our staff and our guests.

COCKTAILS

WHISKY SOUR

The Whisky Sour is one of Marcelo's favourite aperitifs and is therefore a must at DOOR73. A classic that we freshened up with a tangy, velvety foam layer to offset the powerful whisky flavour.

5 cl strong whisky, very lightly peated
2 cl vanilla syrup
2 cl lemon juice
3 drops Angostura bitters
lemon foam

Vanilla syrup
500 ml water
500 g sugar
1 vanilla bean

Sugar syrup
500 ml water
500 g sugar

Lemon foam (for 4 cocktails)
200 ml lemon juice
120 ml sugar syrup
3 g aquafaba

Garnish
Lemon zest

METHOD

For the vanilla syrup:
Put a pan over the heat and bring the water and sugar to a boil. Add a cut-open vanilla bean to the liquid.

For the sugar syrup:
Put a pan over the heat and bring the water and sugar to a boil.

For the lemon foam:
Combine the lemon foam ingredients and beat to a thick foam.

Combine the whisky, vanilla syrup, lemon juice and 3 drops of Angostura bitters in a glass filled with ice.
Stir with a bar spoon to cool and dilute the drink.
Garnish the cocktail with a spoonful of the frothy lemon foam and a strip of lemon zest.

THE BLUE BEAST

This non-alcoholic cocktail was our ironic reaction to a question from one of our guests. 'Do you also have that green cocktail they have at OAK, the one with the foam?' We responded with a bright blue cocktail. Today, contrary to all expectations, The Blue Beast has developed into a crowd favourite, in spite of its simplicity.

6 cl fresh blueberry juice (if you use store-bought juice, make sure the juice contains at least 50 per cent blueberries)
2 cl lemon juice
1.5 cl vanilla syrup
3 cl ginger beer
thyme foam

Thyme foam (for 4 cocktails)
50 ml thyme-infused sugar syrup
100 ml apple juice
50 ml lemon juice
2 g aquafaba

Thyme-infused sugar syrup
500 ml water
500 g sugar
1 bunch fresh thyme
1 pinch citric acid (optional)

Vanilla syrup
500 ml water
500 g sugar
1 vanilla bean

Garnish
grated lime zest
a couple of leaves of fresh thyme

METHOD

For the thyme-infused sugar syrup:
Put a pan over the heat and bring the water and sugar to a boil.
After the liquid has cooled, add a bunch of fresh thyme, together with a pinch of citric acid if desired to strengthen the infusion.

TIP:
Leave the syrup to steep overnight; the longer the infusion steeps, the more intense the flavour. Can't wait that long? Let the thyme infuse in the warm syrup. Bear in mind that the aromas will be less fragrant if you do so.

For the vanilla syrup:
Put a pan over the heat and bring the water and sugar to a boil.
Add a cut-open vanilla bean pod to the liquid.

For the thyme foam:
Combine the thyme foam ingredients and beat to a thick foam.

Combine the blueberry juice, lemon juice and vanilla syrup in a glass filled with ice. Stir to blend all the flavours together.
Top with the ginger beer.

Garnish the cocktail with the frothy foam and lime zest, and finish with a couple of fresh thyme leaves.

NOT A ****** MULE

Given the current geopolitical situation, we have decided to give this classic Mule some southern flair: with passion fruit-infused cachaça, ginger, and lemongrass. In principle, this cocktail is easy to make, but it does take a couple of days to prepare. Your patience will be rewarded.

5 cl passion fruit-infused cachaça
2 cl lemongrass syrup
2 cl lime juice
10 cl ginger beer
10 cl lemongrass essence

Passion fruit-infused cachaça
1 bottle cachaça (max. 1 litre)
500 g passion fruit

Lemongrass syrup
500 ml water
500 g raw cane sugar
5 lemongrass stalks

Lemongrass essence
10 drops lemongrass essential oil
10 cl water

Garnish
1 passion fruit

METHOD

For the passion fruit-infused cachaça:
Use the contents of an entire bottle of cachaça. Thoroughly rinse the passion fruit. Cut the fruit in half and loosen the seeds. Infuse the cachaça with the peel and the pulp for at least 3 days.
Use an airtight container and make sure the passion fruit halves are completely submerged in the cachaça. The longer the infusion steeps, the more intense and complex the flavour.
Strain the liquid through a fine-mesh sieve. Remove the peels and the seeds, but press the moisture out of the pulp and into the infusion while straining the mixture. Use a coffee filter or a muslin cloth to filter out any leftover bits and pieces for optimal flavour.

For the lemongrass syrup:
Put a pan over the heat and bring the water and raw cane sugar to a boil.
Crush and finely chop five lemongrass stalks. Add them to the syrup.
Let simmer covered over low heat so the syrup retains its volatile aromas.
Strain the liquid through a fine-mesh sieve.

For the lemongrass essence:
Add the lemongrass essential oil drops to the water.
Pour the essence into a spray bottle.

Pour the infused cachaça, the lemongrass syrup and the lime juice into a long drink glass filled with ice.
Top with the ginger beer.
Spray the sides of the glass with the lemongrass essence and garnish with fresh passion fruit.

LIQUEUR D'AMOUR

I developed a taste for aniseed and almond after having spent several months in Lebanon. Back in Belgium, I felt homesick for Arak. That's why I went off in search of a cocktail based on these flavours. This liqueur is the result of several failed attempts. This version with cherry reminded me of the Liqueur d'Amour served by Betty, who has been running her homey café in the Patershol in Ghent for years. As she would say: 'Just sit back and enjoy!'

3 cl amaretto
0.5 cl pastis
0.5 cl amaro
1 cl triple sec
1 cl cherry liqueur
5 cl cherry juice

METHOD

Combine all the ingredients and serve chilled in a small glass.

PINEAPPLE PUNCH

This Pineapple Punch is a prime example of how my expertise has grown during my years at DOOR73. It's probably the most complex and technically challenging cocktail on the menu.

10 cl punch (with infused rum)
2 tablespoons lemon verbena foam

Infused rum
400 ml pineapple rum
400 ml cognac
100 ml dark rum
2 star anise
10 cardamom pods
8 allspice berries
12 Sichuan peppers
20 coriander seeds
the peel of 2 lemons

Punch
400 ml sugar syrup (with a ratio of 500 ml water to 500 g sugar)
300 ml lemon juice
300 ml fresh pineapple juice
400 ml full-fat milk

Lemon verbena foam
50 ml lemon-verbena infused sugar syrup (with a ratio of 190 ml water to 65 g sugar and 5 twigs lemon verbena)
1 pinch citric acid
1 egg white

Garnish
1 pineapple slice (fresh or dried)

METHOD

For the infused rum:
Combine the pineapple rum with the cognac and the dark rum.
Combine all the dried ingredients and crush them with a mortar and pestle.
Add the spice mixture to the rum mixture, along with the peels of both lemons.
Heat the mixture sous-vide in a water bath at 65 °C and steep the infusion for 3 hours. For a quicker infusion, you can also use a siphon and keep the ingredients under pressure for 1 1/2 hours.
Pour the cool infusion through a fine mesh sieve.

For the sugar syrup:
Put a pan over the heat and bring the water and sugar to a boil to make the syrup.

For the punch:
To the cooled infused rum, add the sugar syrup, followed by the lemon juice and pineapple juice.
Pour the full-fat milk into a large mixing bowl and slowly add the rum mixture to the milk. Make sure that the milk slowly curdles and sets.
Leave the mixture to rest for several hours.
Pour through a sieve lined with the muslin cloth to filter the liquid.
Pass the mixture through the cloth several times until it is fully transparent. The congealed milk in the muslin cloth acts as an additional filter.
Add the first liquid, which is still cloudy, to the unfiltered batch for a new filter. Do not try to speed up the process; it will take some time before the liquid is fully filtered.

For the lemon verbena foam:
Put a pan over the heat and bring the water and sugar to a boil.
After the liquid has cooled, add the lemon verbena, together with a pinch of citric acid to strengthen the infusion.
Chill the infusion overnight to let it steep.
The following day, mix all the ingredients in a blender and strain through a sieve.
Add an egg white to the infusion and beat to a light foam, with a texture of soap foam.

Pour 10 centilitres of the cooled and clarified punch into a glass filled with a large ice cube.
Top with two spoonfuls of the foam and garnish with a slice of pineapple.

ERIC'S GENEROUS GREEK ROOTS

E My mother, Athina, is not only a professional chef; she also whips up the most delicious dishes at home. She loves Greek classic dishes such as moussaka or a casserole with kritharaki pasta. Although she lives by herself in Crete, she is seldom alone. People drop in all the time unannounced, and she is a gracious hostess to a constant stream of friends and family who stop by for a cup of coffee and a chat. This warm hospitality is typical of those who live in Crete. With her encouragement, I had a wild, carefree childhood. I disappeared after breakfast to go and play football and didn't return home until after sundown, covered in dirt from running around all day. Sitting still was not my strong suit. In fact, I was mainly busy getting up to no good and thinking about what my next meal would look like. I spent most of my time at the beach. On Crete, paying your respects to the sea at least once a day, during breakfast or after work, is a matter of course. I do miss that here sometimes.

Junior master chef

E Because my mother had to work six days a week, my sister Katherina and I had to cook our own meals. My sister didn't mind leaving the cooking to me. I often prepared salads or oven-baked casseroles, following the instructions my mother gave me by phone. Mama felt putting a freshly cooked meal on the table every day was crucial. It's an attitude I have adopted: even when DOOR73's doors are open, I insist on cooking a fresh meal every day after picking up my daughter – we don't do leftovers in my family. When it's possible, I also take plenty of time to make something delicious; I can easily spend up to 3 hours in the kitchen. My dishes are always inspired by Greek cuisine in some way, even if it's just a tiny detail. In fact, I'm completely mad about the Cretan food culture. We are big eaters, and we'd eat throughout the day if we could. Because Crete is an island, we often work with local fish, but meat also plays an important role: goats and sheep graze on the mountainside, and pigs are often kept. My father was the one who introduced me to the world of meat and protein-rich dishes. In Crete, it's normal to go out into the White Mountains and pick herbs such as oregano, marjoram, and chamomile to season traditional Greek stews. In terms of vegetables, our cuisine is distinguished by its use of tomato, aubergine, courgette, red beetroot, and cabbage. Most community centres in Crete are traditionally equipped with a seasonal vegetable garden; some even have an olive grove where families can press their own olive oil. To grow up in such a rich environment is relatively unique. Crete's landscape is so varied: within an hour, you can travel from cities to rocky ravines, snow-capped mountains, and pristine shores. Today, the island is popular with artists and businessmen who come to revive family businesses, renovate historical buildings, or modernise vineyards. And yet, much has changed. My earliest childhood memories include days when I would go fishing with my father. Today, it's strange to pass by those spots and conclude that everyone, both the fish population and the fishing community, has gone. I crave that simplicity and purity. That's why I won't abandon the idea of one day buying a boat of my own to relive that experience.

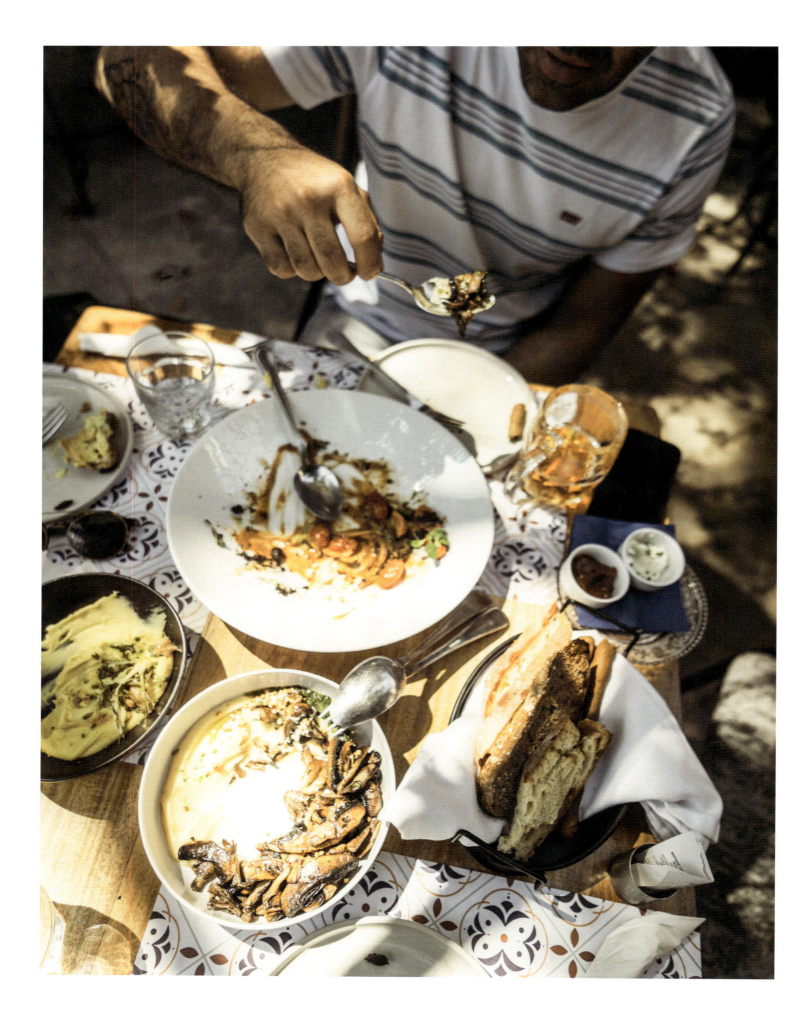

The search for a culinary adventure

E I helped my father during my teenage years at the construction sites where he worked, but the work didn't interest me much. When I was 15 years old, I decided to earn a little extra money as a waiter. And again, I was overcome by boredom. Still, this period allowed me to come into contact with the chefs and the typical kitchen dynamic in an informal setting. I was fascinated by what they did but didn't truly realise how challenging those working conditions were. In Crete, the temperature is a near-constant 40°C, and in the kitchens – especially kitchens working with open fire as opposed to induction – temperatures skyrocketed. Intrigued by kitchen life, at the age of 17 I decided to risk crossing to the mainland in order to start my education in Athens as a chef. I worked double shifts at local restaurants at the weekends to help finance my costly studies. After graduation, I hung around a bit until I felt it was time to apply for traineeships abroad. During the touristy summer season, I worked in Crete and Rhodes. And by the time I had any free time, the summer and my friends all seemed to have disappeared. It felt constricting. I applied for traineeships at a three-star and a one-star restaurant, hoping to find a different course in life. And when I was finally given the green light from a three-star restaurant in Spain, I panicked. I suddenly felt I was too young and inexperienced. That's how I eventually ended up at Pure C in Cadzand at the age of 24. Little did I know that the bar would be raised just as high. And thankfully, they kept me so busy that there wasn't any time left for me to bemoan the fact.

One particularly valuable relationship from my studies in Athens remains with me today. That's where I met my mentor, Fanis Stathis, who taught me that you must work hard to achieve something. Anyone who works in the restaurant sector for the money has chosen the wrong profession. He was convinced that as long as you strive for perfection, success will automatically follow. And he was right. It's all about having a vision. You can only keep this up by remaining focused. I remember calling him from Cadzand and telling him I had to work 16 hours a day. 'And? Is that all?' I heard on the other end of the line. His response surprised me, but I now know better: there is no shortcut to success.

My wife Eleni comes from Rhodes, and I am a Cretan by birth. Both Greek islands are very proud of their roots, and Cretans even more so; they consider themselves demigods. We are a very passionate people and can sometimes be very eccentric. When discussing something with my sous-chefs in our kitchen, I get so passionate that people think we're arguing when, in fact, that's just the way we communicate in Crete. With hindsight, Eleni and I took a risk leaving our homeland for a backwater like Cadzand without a plan B to fall back on, but we didn't give it a second thought. Today, I travel to Greece twice a year to visit my family. And food continues to be the central theme for my reunions. My sister's husband, for instance, owns a pita restaurant; I'm always called in to try the latest additions to the menu. Or I need a recipe from my mother because I'm stuck working on a new dish. She always knows what to do.

STARTERS

RED BEETROOT TZATZIKI

Preparation time: 1 hour   Serves 4

This version of tzatziki is an absolute winner on a weekend day off; that's how Marcelo and I get the most out of it. Personally, I'm a huge fan of summertime beetroot, especially when they are extra sweet from the sunshine. To illustrate how versatile beetroot can be, I work with both raw and cooked beets grated to a fine texture.

30 g beetroot
100 g Greek-style yoghurt
2 g salt
10 ml olive oil
4 ml Chardonnay vinegar
10 g pickled mustard seeds
1 g garlic
10 g raw beetroot, grated
1 slice sourdough bread
20 g feta
1 g oregano
splash of olive oil

Pickled mustard seeds
50 g mustard seeds
50 g sugar
100 ml white wine vinegar
50 ml water

METHOD

For the pickled mustard seeds:
Put all the ingredients in a pot and simmer for 3 minutes.
Set aside to chill in the refrigerator.

Wrap the beetroot in aluminium foil and place in the oven at 180 °C for 45 minutes to 1 hour until soft and tender. Peel and finely grate the beetroot.
Add all the ingredients, except for the bread, the feta, the oregano and the olive oil, together in a bowl.
Spoon a generous spoonful of tzatziki onto a plate or into a bowl.
Serve the tzatziki with a slice of sourdough bread topped with crumbled feta, a splash of olive oil and some oregano.

BRIOCHE WITH CHICKEN MOUSSE

Preparation time: 1 hour   Serves 2

At the restaurant, I have noticed that guests are often hesitant when it comes to eating organ meats. They always react with delighted surprise when they discover afterwards that I have used chicken livers in a dish. This homemade brioche with chicken mousse is a wintry classic that also involves pickled beetroot and blueberry jelly. Personally, I think this dish is a fabulous combination of textures.

80 g chicken liver mousse
70 g brioche
20 g pickles
20 g pickled beetroot
10 g blueberry jelly
10 g glazed onion
2 g Maldon salt

Pickled beetroot
100 ml vinegar
50 g sugar
50 ml water
100 g red beetroot slices

Chicken liver mousse
100 g bacon
200 g white onions
50 g shallots
100 ml white port
100 ml madeira wine
50 ml calvados
500 g chicken livers
200 g eggs
1 egg yolk
200 g clarified butter
16 g salt

Glazed onion
140 ml Chardonnay vinegar
60 g sugar
50 ml maple syrup
40 g butter
100 g shallots, halved

Blueberry jelly
200 g blueberries
100 ml water
10 ml lemon juice
4 g agar

Brioche
4 eggs
100 ml milk
500 g T65 flour
10 g salt
20 g yeast
60 g granulated sugar
220 g butter
1 egg yolk
20 ml water

METHOD

For the pickled beetroot:
Add the vinegar, sugar and water to a saucepan and bring to a boil. Set aside to chill in the refrigerator. Add the red beetroot slices and store the pickle at least 12 hours in the refrigerator before use.

For the glazed onion:
Combine all the ingredients in a saucepan and simmer to a glaze. Remove the shallots from the pan.

For the blueberry jelly:
Combine all the ingredients in a pan and cook for 2 minutes. Put the mixture into another pan and let it cool until it sets. Transfer the jelly to a blender and mix until creamy.

For the brioche:
Use a hand mixer with a dough hook attachment. Combine the eggs with the milk in a bowl at the lowest speed setting. Add the flour, the salt and the yeast. Mix for another 2 minutes to combine the ingredients into a homogenous whole. Stop mixing and scrape the sides of the bowl. Increase the speed setting on your mixer and mix for another 2 minutes. With the mixer turning at high speed, slowly and gradually stir in the granulated sugar. Make sure the sugar has dissolved before adding more — the entire process should take up about 5 minutes. As the sugar is incorporated in the dough, it will come away from the sides of the bowl. Add all the butter. Mix for an additional 10 minutes at high speed until the butter is fully incorporated. Scrape the bowl clean at least once during this process. The dough will start to lump around the hooks and will come away from the sides of the bowl with a slight beating sound. Check to see if the dough is shiny, smooth and moist. If it is, then your dough is ready. Grease a large bowl with cooking spray. Roll the dough around in the bowl so it is fully coated with the spray. Cover the bowl with cling film. Leave the dough in a warm spot (between 25 and 30 °C) for one hour. Coat your workbench with a thin layer of flour, remove the dough from the bowl and place it on your work surface. Carefully fold the dough into three parts, like folding a letter. Turn the dough 90° and fold again in the same way. Then return the dough to the bowl, cover the bowl and leave to prove for another 30 minutes. Store the dough in the refrigerator for 12 hours. Roll out into 80-gram pieces. Place the pieces in small baking tins, brush a layer of lightly beaten egg yolk (mixed with water) over the top and leave the mini brioches to prove for 30-40 minutes. Bake the brioche for 12 minutes in an oven preheated to 180 °C and leave to cool before serving.

For the chicken liver mousse:
Fry the bacon in a pan until cooked through, then add the onions and shallots. Sauté the onions until soft. Then add all the alcohol and continue to cook until the alcohol has evaporated. Leave the mixture to chill in the refrigerator. Put 250 g of the mixture into a blender. Add the liver, the eggs and the egg yolk and blend into a smooth cream. Strain through a sieve and return to the blender. Blend while slowly adding the clarified butter until the mixture turns to mayonnaise. Add salt and spoon the mousse into an airtight container. Steam the mousse for 2 hours at 65 °C before leaving it in the refrigerator for 12 hours.

Transfer the chicken liver mousse to a piping bag and pipe a dollop onto a plate.

Arrange some finely chopped pickles and three small dollops of the blueberry jelly on top. Then heat the brioche for 3 minutes in an oven at 180 °C and add the glazed onion. Garnish with the pickled beets and Maldon salt.

How do you know if your dough has been kneaded long enough?
Do the windowpane test. Take a small amount of dough, flatten it between your thumb and index finger and very gently pull the dough on opposite ends until it's almost translucent. The dough should not be allowed to tear. If it does tear, knead the dough for an additional 3 minutes and try again.

KALITSOUNIA PASTY

〰️ Preparation time: 5 hours   👤 Serves 6

This kalitsounia pasty recipe is an ode to my roots. And, with this nostalgic version, I want to make sure that the traditional recipe will never be lost. The traditional recipe specifically calls for mizithra cheese. A bite of this crunchy pasty reminds me of happy snacking moments when I was a young boy. As for the cream filling, that's completely up to you: cheese, spinach... Personally, I'm partial to the sweet and sour flavour palette of sheep and goat cheese with honey.

500 g T55 flour
45 ml olive oil
45 ml Cretan raki (or grappa)
250 ml water
5 g salt
500 g mizithra cheese (or ricotta)
200 g grated tyromalama cheese (or Gouda)
10 g mint
20 g corn flour
1 egg
3 g salt
1 egg yolk
20 ml water
5 g sesame seeds

METHOD

Combine the flour, the olive oil, the raki, the water and the salt in a bowl and knead for 5 minutes.
Leave the dough to rest for 30 minutes before repeating the kneading process.
Set the dough aside to rest in the refrigerator for 3 hours.
Use a rolling pin to roll the dough out into a thin layer and then cut it into squares or circles. Fold them into an envelope shape.

Preheat the oven to 180 °C.
Make the filling by combining the cheeses, the mint, the corn flour, the egg and the salt together.
Fill one of the dough circles or squares with the filling.
Brush a layer of beaten egg yolk (mixed with water) over the dough and close the dough like you would seal an envelope.
Finish with another layer of beaten egg yolk with some sesame seeds sprinkled over the top.
Bake the pasties in a preheated oven for 20 to 25 minutes and serve warm.

GRILLED CORN ON THE COB WITH TOMATO BUTTER AND PARMESAN

◇ Preparation time: 30 minutes 👤 Serves 2

This dish has Italian roots written all over it. I clearly remember how this ended up on DOOR73's menu. One of us had eaten grilled sweetcorn on the cob in Copenhagen and was duly impressed. Although I wasn't sure whether it would be a hit among our guests — I was afraid that they would find it a bit too corny — everyone loved it. The glaze, made with sundried tomatoes and Parmesan cheese, gives this sweetcorn its savoury flavour.

2 ears of fresh sweetcorn
2 litres boiling water
50 g salt
50 g sugar
100 g butter

20 g tomato powder
50 g Parmesan cheese, grated
10 ml olive oil
1 g pepper
2 g salt

METHOD

Cook the ears of sweetcorn for 20 min. in boiling water containing the dissolved salt and sugar.
Soften the butter, add 10 g of tomato powder and 20 g of grated Parmesan cheese. Grill the cooked sweetcorn on all sides in olive oil until the ears have that lovely golden colour.
Coat the sweetcorn with the butter and season with the salt and pepper, the remaining Parmesan cheese and the tomato powder.

HOLSTEIN TONNATO

〰️ Preparation time: 2 to 3 hours   👤 Serves 4

This twist on vitello tonnato has graced our menu for the longest during DOOR 73's rich history. With my version, I want to explore how far I can go with this dish without having it lose its distinctive character. The most distinctive element in this dish is the bread soufflé, something I picked up from the kitchen at Pure C. This Holstein tonnato has become my signature dish over the years. Guests come and visit for this dish alone, and that is why I feel it is important that all my trainees learn to prepare this during their traineeship.

40 g mustard greens
1 g Maldon salt
20 ml olive oil
10 ml Cabernet Sauvignon vinegar
10 g capers
80 g smoked Holstein beef, sliced
60 g tuna mayonnaise
10 g pickled mustard seeds
40 g bread soufflé

Tuna mayonnaise
50 g egg yolk
15 g Dijon mustard
125 g canned tuna
5 g salt
20 ml Cabernet Sauvignon vinegar
300 ml maize oil

Bread soufflé
320 g T00 flour
20 g yeast
190 ml milk
5 g salt

Pickled mustard seeds
50 g mustard seeds
50 g sugar
100 ml white wine vinegar
50 ml water

METHOD

For the tuna mayonnaise:
Combine all the ingredients except for the oil in a blender and mix.
Slowly add the oil until you obtain a creamy mayonnaise.
Let the mayonnaise rest in the refrigerator for an hour.

For the bread soufflé:
Knead all the ingredients together in a food processor, then let the dough rest for 30 mins.
Knead the dough once more for 1 minute before leaving it to rest for another 30 mins.
Feed the dough through a pasta machine at thickness setting 6 (3 mm thick).
Cut out circles with a diameter of 10 cm and bake them in a preheated oven at 250 °C for 3 minutes until golden brown.

For the pickled mustard seeds:
Put all the ingredients in a pot and simmer for 3 minutes.
Set aside to chill in the refrigerator.

Marinate the mustard greens in the salt, the olive oil and the Cabernet Sauvignon vinegar.
Deep-fry the capers at 160 °C until all the moisture has been removed. Drain the capers on kitchen paper.
Place a couple of slices of smoked Holstein on a plate and garnish with the fried capers.
Top the beef with the bread soufflé filled with the tuna mayonnaise.
Arrange the remaining beef slices on top and finish with the pickled mustard seeds.
Serve with the prepared greens as a side.

CHICKEN WINGS WITH BARBECUE SAUCE AND AIOLI

Preparation time: 35 minutes Serves 4

At Syrco Bakker's Food Fest in Cadzand, Marcelo and I served the ultimate festival snack: chicken wings. I have fine-tuned the recipe for my barbecue sauce just for this book.

500 g chicken wings
5 g salt
50 ml olive oil
1 g chilli powder
10 g smoked paprika powder
40 g tortilla chips
100 ml barbecue sauce
60 g aioli

Barbecue sauce
140 ml tomato ketchup
120 ml apple cider
120 ml soy sauce
100 g brown sugar
30 g treacle
25 ml Worcestershire sauce
20 g tomato paste
10 g salt
5 g celery seeds
5 g garlic powder
5 g cumin
5 g black pepper
2 g onion powder
2 g smoked paprika powder
0.5 g cayenne pepper

Aioli
50 g garlic confit
100 g egg yolk
9 ml Chardonnay vinegar
1 g fresh garlic
60 ml water
700 ml maize oil

METHOD

For the barbecue sauce:
Whisk all the ingredients together in a small saucepan. Bring to a boil over medium heat, stirring regularly so the sugar dissolves nicely and the sauce doesn't burn. Simmer for 15 mins. Remove the pan from the heat as soon as the sauce has reduced to the right consistency and cover. Let the sauce cool to room temperature; this should take about 30 minutes. Transfer the sauce to an airtight container. You can store this sauce in the refrigerator for up to 3 weeks.

For the aioli:
Combine all the ingredients except for the oil. Slowly add the oil until you obtain a creamy mayonnaise.

For the chicken wings:
Marinate the chicken wings in a bowl containing the salt, the olive oil, the chilli powder and the smoked paprika powder for 30 minutes. Place the marinated chicken wings on a tray and cover with aluminium foil. Bake the wings for 20 mins. in an oven preheated to 180 °C. Remove the chicken wings from the oven and baste them in the sauce. Return them to the oven for another 3 to 4 minutes — raise the temperature to 200 °C this time, allowing the chicken wings to caramelise. Garnish with the tortilla chips and serve the aioli on the side as a dipping sauce.

TIRADITO DE PESCADO

Preparation time: 2 hours   Serves 2-4

A tiradito is the Peruvian little brother of ceviche. This dish is based on market-fresh raw whitefish — I use sea bream — sliced into sashimi and marinated just before serving with a tangy citrus-shellfish dressing. This dish packs a punch thanks to the fruity, spicy flavours released by the aji amarillo chilli pepper.

150 g sea bream
3 g salt
1 g lemon zest
20 ml olive oil
50 g avocado cream
20 g cape gooseberry
5 g Thai red chilli
10 g coriander
60 ml tiradito juice

Avocado cream
100 g avocado
10 ml lime juice
7 g coriander

15 g Greek-style yoghurt
7 ml sushi vinegar
3 g salt
15 ml olive oil
3 drops Tabasco sauce

Tiradito juice
40 g cape gooseberry
15 g aji amarillo chilli pepper
525 ml lime juice
350 g red onions
5 g Thai red chilli
6 g garlic

75 g fresh coriander
5 g salt
250 ml shellfish juice

Shellfish juice
50 ml maize oil
10 g garlic, minced
500 g mussels
500 g razor clams
500 g clams
200 ml white wine
salt

METHOD

For the shellfish juice:
Put a medium pan with the maize oil over heat. Add and sauté the garlic. After 1 minute, add all the shellfish, followed by the white wine and a pinch of salt. Cover the pan and cook everything for 10 minutes over low heat until all the shells are open. Pour the juice through a fine mesh sieve.

For the tiradito juice:
Blend the cape gooseberries, the chillies and the lime juice in a blender. Peel the red onions and roughly chop them into uniform pieces. Roughly chop the red pepper, garlic and coriander. Combine the chopped red onion, coriander, red chilli pepper and garlic together with the salt in a bowl. Then add the shellfish juice and lime-cape gooseberry mixture to the bowl. Cover and leave overnight in the refrigerator. The following day, pour the juice through a fine mesh sieve and use immediately.

For the avocado cream:
Combine all the ingredients into a creamy blend.
Slice the sea bream and add the salt, lemon zest and olive oil. Arrange the slices on a plate. Add the avocado cream and gooseberries together with the finely chopped red chillies and coriander. Finish with the tiradito juice and olive oil.

Serving tip:
Serve with cuttlefish crackers, available at any Asian grocery store.

TARAMA WITH SUMAC AND CHIVE OIL

〰️ Preparation time: 15 minutes   👤 Serves 4-6

This recipe for tarama — typical of the Greek culinary tradition — lies close to my heart. I got the basic recipe from my mother, but with a touch of Asian spice and the distinctive green oil, I gave this addictively delicious dip my personal touch. I serve this dip as a first amuse-bouche to every guest as DOOR73, just to highlight how important this recipe is to me. I consider this to be the perfect introduction to who I am and how I approach cooking. Many people believe that making tarama is simply a matter of mixing together a couple of ingredients, but every truly delicious tarama requires a lot more work. Moreover, I find that the texture of tarama is often too creamy. The combination of sumac and chives gave me just the right balance I was looking for.

250 ml maize oil
70 g white onions
70 g cod roe (ask at your local fishmonger)
130 ml water
75 g panko
2 g salt

10 ml lemon juice
1 g sumac
20 ml chive oil

Chive oil
300 g chives
900 ml maize oil

METHOD

Put a small pan with the maize oil over heat and sauté the minced onions over medium heat. Make sure they turn soft but never cook completely through.
Combine all the ingredients except for sumac and chive oil in a blender. Blend the ingredients until smooth.

For the chive oil:
Heat the maize oil in a small saucepan to 70 °C.
Finely chop the chives in a blender and add them to the oil. Deep-fry the chives very briefly before removing the pan from heat.
Pour the oil mixture through a sieve. The chive oil will keep for up to 1 month after it has cooled.

Slowly add the maize oil to your mixture and blend to a nice, creamy consistency (like hummus).
Put a spoonful of tarama onto a plate or into a bowl.
Garnish the tarama with sumac and chive oil.

Serving tip:
Spread the tarama on a slice of crispy sourdough toast for optimal flavour.

RICOTTA WITH DRIED DATE TOMATOES AND CAPER

◇◇◇ Preparation time: 6 hours   👤 Serves 4

Few people realise that caper leaves — after they have been salted and pickled in a specific way — are actually edible. Greece is home to several farms that specialise in this time-honoured tradition. I use ricotta, which gives this recipe an Italian touch, but feel free to experiment with feta, burrata… What is essential to this dish are the sweet and sour date tomatoes that burst with flavour when in season.

200 g dried date tomatoes
60 g ricotta
10 ml olive oil
1 g oregano
20 g feta
15 g croutons
8 to 10 caper leaves
20 ml spring onion oil
1 g lemon zest
40 ml tomato juice dressing

Spring onion oil
100 g spring onions
300 ml maize oil

Tomato juice dressing
2 tomatoes
10 ml white balsamic vinegar
20 ml olive oil
1 g salt

Croutons
1 slice sourdough bread
50 ml olive oil
1 g garlic
1 g pepper
2 g salt

METHOD

Preheat the oven to 60 °C. Bring a medium-sized pot filled with water to the boil. Blanch the tomatoes for 6 seconds in the boiling water. Then submerge them in a bowl of iced water. Peel off the skins. Dry the tomatoes for 4 to 6 hours in the oven. Meanwhile, puree the ricotta together with the olive oil and the oregano.

For the spring onion oil:
Use a stick blender to blend the onions with the oil. Heat the mixture in a saucepan before straining the mixture through a sieve.

For the tomato juice dressing:
Blend two fresh tomatoes and press them through a fine mesh sieve to collect the juice. Add vinegar, olive oil and salt to taste to the tomato juice.

For the croutons:
Preheat the oven to 180 °C. Dice a slice of sourdough bread into small cubes (aim for about 15 grams' worth of croutons). Add olive oil, garlic, pepper and salt and bake for 6 to 8 minutes in the oven until the croutons are nice and crispy.

Use a cooking ring to compose your plate.
Start with a layer of ricotta, then add the croutons, the caper leaves, the spring onion oil and the dried date tomatoes. Finish with salt, pepper, lemon zest and the tomato juice dressing.

SOFT-SHELL CRAB TEMPURA WITH WASABI MAYONNAISE

〰️ Preparation time: 1 hour   👤 Serves 2-4

I was stewing over this dish for months until one of my fellow chefs gave me the ultimate recipe for perfect crispy tempura batter. Many tempuras have the tendency to lose their crispiness after a while. Please note: this is a rich dish because you deep-fry the tempura à la minute, but also because of the use of the vinegar dressing and the wasabi mayonnaise.

50 g quinoa
1 litre water
10 g salt
40 g cucumber, diced into small cubes
40 g wasabi mayonnaise
20 g daikon
1 soft-shell crab
400 ml oil for deep frying
30 g tempura
1 sheet of nori
40 ml dashi vinegar dressing

Dashi vinegar dressing
100 ml Tosazu/dashi vinegar
50 ml soy sauce
100 ml sushi vinegar
30 ml olive oil

Tempura
700 ml iced water
380 g tempura flour
4 g salt
20 g egg yolk
50 g flour

Wasabi mayonnaise
100 g egg yolk
40 g wasabi paste
20 ml sushi vinegar
20 g sugar
6 g salt
50 ml water
600 ml maize oil

METHOD

For the dashi vinegar dressing:
Combine all the ingredients and finish with a splash of olive oil.

For the tempura:
Beat all the ingredients into a smooth mixture in a bowl with a hand mixer; make sure the batter doesn't have any lumps.

For the wasabi mayonnaise:
Put all the ingredients except for the maize oil in a blender and blend. Slowly add the olive oil to form a smooth mayonnaise.

Cook the quinoa in salted water for 10-12 minutes, drain the quinoa and briefly set aside.
Combine the diced cucumber with the quinoa and half the wasabi mayonnaise.
Add a pinch of salt and season the mixture to taste.
Then slice the daikon into strips with a mandolin slicer and arrange them in a circle on the plate. Place the quinoa-cucumber salad in the middle of the circle.
Coat the crab by dipping it in the tempura.
Fry the crab for 2 minutes in a deep fryer preheated to 160 °C. Remove the crab from the deep fryer and let it drain on kitchen paper.
Garnish the salad with a pinch of salt and the remaining wasabi mayonnaise. Place the crab on top. Top with the nori and sprinkle the dashi vinegar dressing over the top.

PAN DE CRISTAL WITH FRIED SARDINES

△△△ Preparation time: 45 minutes   👤 Serves 2-4

Pan de cristal, also known as glass bread, is a grossly underrated Spanish delicacy. I have Spanish friends who encourage me to work with artisanal products from Spain; and I often have to agree with them. And yet, the idea for this particular dish comes from my Greek mother. She encouraged me to wrap sardines in grape leaves. And I'm not exaggerating when I say that when you serve these on Pan de Cristal, you're going to discover a Mediterranean flavour bomb.

200 g grape leaves, salted
400 g sardines
20 ml olive oil
100 g tarama
200 g pan de cristal
1 g Maldon salt
40 ml lime dressing
salt

Tarama
250 ml maize oil
70 g white onions
70 g cod roe (ask at your local fishmonger)

130 ml water
75 g panko
2 g salt
10 ml lemon juice
1 g sumac

Lime dressing
40 g lime pulp
20 ml olive oil
1 g salt

METHOD

For the tarama:
Put a small pan with the maize oil over heat and sauté the minced onions over medium heat. Make sure they turn soft but never cook completely through.
Combine all the ingredients except for the sumac in a blender. Blend the ingredients until smooth.
Slowly add the maize oil to your mixture and blend to a nice, creamy consistency (like hummus).
Garnish the tarama with sumac.

For the sardines:
Wash the grape leaves and pat them dry with kitchen paper.
Clean the sardines thoroughly as well; remove the backbone, but leave the tails on.

Sprinkle salt over the sardines.
Place each sardine on a grape leaf and roll the leaf up.
Add olive oil to a pan and fry each side of the sardine for 1 minute; the sardine should still be slightly pink on the inside.

For the pan de cristal:
Preheat the oven to 180 °C.
Slice the pan de cristal into a long rectangular shape and sprinkle with olive oil.
Bake the bread in the oven for 5 to 7 minutes until golden brown and crispy.
Garnish with Maldon salt.

For the lime dressing:
Cut lime wedges away from the skin and finely chop the pulp. Add a bit of olive oil and salt.
Combine to make the dressing.

Spread tarama on a piece of oven-baked pan de cristal, arrange the wrapped sardines on top and sprinkle with the lime dressing.

FRIED ARTICHOKES

≈≈≈ Preparation time: 1 hour   👤 Serves 4

The French-Belgian way to serve artichoke with a mustard dressing is delicious, but I am more enthralled with the Italian approach, which involves making a dried powder from red onions, deep frying the artichoke and then combining it with the tangy flavour of stracciatella.

1 artichoke
500 ml oil for deep frying
2 g salt
1 g pepper
60 g stracciatella cheese
10 ml ramson oil
red onion powder

Red onion powder
500 g red onions

Ramson oil
300 g ramsons (wild garlic)
900 ml maize oil

METHOD

For the red onion powder:
Preheat the oven to 160 °C.
Thinly slice the onion, spread the slices out over a baking tray and cover with aluminium foil. Bake them for 20 minutes in the oven until soft.
Put the onions in a baking dish and bake at 40 °C until they are completely dry; this process may take up to 10 hours. Using a wooden spoon, wedge the oven door ajar (about 3 cm).
Put the dried onions in the blender and blend to a fine powder.

For the ramson oil:
Add the ingredients to a Thermomix and let them cook at 80 °C for 4 minutes. Pass the oil through a sieve.

Clean and trim the outside of the artichoke with a knife and then spoon out the choke. Make sure all the prickly fibres have been removed.
Deep-fry the artichoke for 4 to 5 minutes at 160 °C until soft. Check for doneness with a fork.
Remove the artichoke from the deep fryer and let it drain on kitchen paper.
Place the artichoke on a plate, add salt and pepper, and finally the stracciatella, the ramson oil and the red onion powder.

SHELLFISH À LA TAIWAN

Preparation time: 20 minutes   Serves 4

When Marcelo travelled to Taiwan with his sous-chef, Nick, and his sommelier, Valerie, he ate the most amazing clams. He felt that those clams were a perfect addition to DOOR73's menu. The finely chopped Thai basil makes all the difference. This dish is delightfully easy to make, but at the same time brings out the most intense flavours.

30 g butter
2 g garlic
250 g clams or cockles
50 ml white wine
10 g dark soy sauce
10 g Thai basil, finely chopped
pinch of black pepper
10 ml lime juice

METHOD

Put a small pan on the heat, add the butter and the garlic and sauté for 1 minute. Add the shellfish, followed by the wine and the soy sauce.
Cook the shellfish until they are all open and garnish with finely chopped Thai basil and pepper. Serve them in a bowl and drizzle a bit of lime juice over the top.

BROTHERS IN CRIME

M   When I met Eric at Pure C, I thought he looked like a caveman. He was very crude and macho in his ways. And yet, we soon developed a bond. Perhaps because we were the only 'foreigners' in the kitchen and he always needed a ride home, as we shared a house in the neighbourhood. I oversaw the cold kitchen, where he worked as a trainee. Chef Syrco Bakker called Eric Tiki – a shortened version of tzatziki – and I was referred to as Ronaldo, after the famous footballer. The atmosphere was informal, with plenty of room for horsing around but sufficiently serious for when we needed to get down to business. This balance was critical; our team of eight chefs provided meals for a thousand guests each week. One of my most memorable moments was when Eric was offered a permanent contract at the restaurant – as if I instinctively felt fate had brought us together.

E   The first time I felt homesick was three months into my traineeship at Pure C. When I told Marcelo that I wanted to leave, he stopped me. Maybe he was afraid that my work would then land on his shoulders. Syrco also did his best to make me stay. Eleni was taken on board to provide breakfast for the hotel guests and help out with the service at Pure C. When I saw how much everyone was enjoying themselves, I decided to stay. When I look back upon those times, I think our period there was instrumental in determining the course our lives would take. Marcelo and I can take rough handling, so to speak. The Dutch are incredibly direct and just a bit crazy, something we found out at the best and worst of times.

Everyone belongs to the world

E   Our shared sense of humour and sunny, southern roots – Brazilian in his case, Greek in mine – led to an instant bond. This doesn't mean that we were treated as outsiders by our colleagues, but we felt that shared bond very strongly. And because we both had a different country of birth, we very consciously and explicitly chose this region. Belgians are open to discovery. If they're not familiar with a certain ingredient or want to learn more about a specific sauce, dip, or dressing, they'll instantly start asking questions. Dining out has more than just a functional aspect: Belgians go out for dinner to celebrate. And that mindset is a gift from heaven for chefs. We are only a part of the bigger picture and contribute in our own small way to the identity of Ghent, Flanders, Belgium, and Europe. We are proud to be a part of that culinary community. I feel welcomed and supported here.

M   Just like Eric, I am incredibly thankful for being able to start a business as a chef here in Belgium. Belgian restaurant goers breathe gastronomy. Belgium is – and I'm not exaggerating here – the best place in the world to own a restaurant. Belgians love dining out. Every day is a blessing when one is allowed to cook for such guests. At OAK, almost everyone orders the most extensive menu without batting an eyelid. That exuberant aspect of dining out and celebrating life together is part of their national character. During my travels, I feel as much like a Belgian as a cosmopolitan.

MOUSSAKA

Preparation time: 2 hours   Serves 4

Greek moussaka is without a doubt the most popular dish from my homeland. It forms the culinary heart of every tavern and every family celebration. You could think of moussaka as an inherent part of our culture, a meal that brings generations together. Below you'll find my favourite version of this classic.

3 medium-sized aubergines
 (sliced into 6 x 0.5 cm slices)
550 g Maris Piper potatoes
 (sliced into 6 x 0.5 cm slices)
60 ml olive oil
800 g mixed minced meat
 (70% beef, 30% pork)
150 g onion, finely chopped
salt
20 g garlic, minced
5 g oregano
2 cinnamon sticks
10 g allspice
2 bay leaves
200 ml red wine
400 g canned chopped tomatoes
2 tablespoons tomato paste
30 g pecorino cheese
100 ml béchamel sauce
60 g Emmental cheese

Béchamel sauce
40 g unsalted butter
40 g flour
450 ml full-fat milk
40 g Parmesan cheese, finely grated
5 g grated nutmeg
4 g salt
0.5 g pepper
1 g garlic powder
1 egg
1 egg yolk (lightly beaten)

METHOD

Deep-fry the aubergines until golden brown in colour or bake them (in a dish greased with olive oil) in a preheated oven at 180 °C.
Deep-fry the potatoes until golden brown and soft.
Drain them on kitchen paper.
Heat 1 tablespoon oil in a large ovenproof cooking pot or saucepan over medium heat.
Add the minced meat and fry for 8 to 10 minutes until golden brown, stirring regularly and breaking the mince up into smaller chunks with a wooden spoon.
Spoon the meat into a bowl and set aside.
Add the remaining oil to the pot or pan.
Add the onion and a pinch of salt and sauté for 10 to 12 minutes over low heat until the onions are soft and translucent.
Then add the garlic, oregano, cinnamon, chilli pepper, allspice and bay leaf and sauté for another minute.
Spoon the meat back into the pan and add the red wine.
Bring the contents to a simmer and reduce the wine by half.
Stir the tomatoes, tomato paste and 200 ml water into the pot.
Lower the heat and let simmer uncovered for 20 minutes.
Stir regularly until the sauce has thickened.

For the béchamel sauce:
Melt the butter in a small saucepan, stir the flour in and cook over medium-high heat for 1 minute.
Remove the pan from heat and gradually whisk in the milk to form a smooth sauce.
Put the pan back over the heat and gently simmer the sauce for 3 minutes.
Remove the pan from heat once more and whisk in the Parmesan cheese, the grated nutmeg, salt, pepper, garlic and some fresh green herbs if desired (coriander, parsley or dill).
Finally, add the whole egg and the beaten egg yolk.

Arrange the fried potatoes on the bottom of a large, rectangular ovenproof dish.
Cover the potatoes with half the meat mixture, spreading it as thinly as possible.
Arrange a layer of aubergine slices on top, followed by the remaining meat mixture, the pecorino and another layer of aubergine.
Add a little bit of Parmesan, salt and fresh pepper.
Pour the béchamel sauce over the top, add the Emmental cheese and bake in the oven at 200 °C until the sauce turns golden brown.
Let the moussaka set for an hour before cutting it into pieces.
Garnish with some leftover cheese before serving.

BRAISED LAMB SHANKS

◆ Preparation time: 2 hours   👤 Serves 2-4

Lamb is a very popular meat in Greece. The earthy flavours of natural lamb contribute to the rich flavour of these braised shanks. The lamb broth also manages to add an extra savoury touch. This particular dish takes me back to the mountains of Crete.

2 lamb shanks, excess fat removed
2 tablespoons olive oil
2 large carrots, cut into 1 1/2-cm pieces
1 large white onion, diced
6 garlic cloves, minced
1 teaspoon coarse salt
1/2 teaspoon freshly ground pepper
400 ml lamb broth

Lamb broth
1 cup red wine
200 g passata
2 tablespoons tomato paste
1 teaspoon fresh rosemary, finely chopped
2 tablespoons fresh parsley, finely chopped
2 bay leaves
1 litre lamb stock

Lamb stock
2 kg lamb bones
a dash of oil
1 tablespoon of butter
6 white onions, finely chopped
500 g carrots, finely sliced
2 whole heads of garlic, cut in half
1 small bunch of thyme, chopped
1 tablespoon whole black peppercorns
1 tablespoon coriander seeds
500 g red port
100 g cognac
salt and pepper

METHOD:

For the lamb stock
Preheat the oven to 220°C and roast the lamb bones in it until they are a nice golden brown. Put a pressure cooker with the oil and butter over medium heat. Roast the onions, carrots, and all of the herbs and spices in the oil and butter. Deglaze with the port and cognac, and flambé. Let the liquid boil. Add the bones when the liquid has reduced. Cover the bones with water. Close the lid of the pressure cooker and let it cook for 2 hours. If you don't have a pressure cooker, let it simmer for 12 hours over low heat.
Allow the stock to cool overnight in a cool place. The next morning, skim off the hard layer of fat and throw it away. Strain the liquid through a sieve. Let the liquid boil down until the lamb stock is the right thickness. Season with salt and pepper.

For the lamb broth:
Reduce the wine until all the alcohol has evaporated.
Add the passata, the tomato paste, lamb stock and the herbs.
Cover and simmer for 2 1/2 hours on the bottom rack of the oven.

Remove the bay leaves from the sauce and return the pot to the heat.
Reduce the sauce over medium heat until it has reached the desired consistency.
The sauce should be thick enough to cover the back of a spoon with a thin film.

For the lamb shanks:
Preheat the oven to 175 °C.
Rinse the lamb shanks and pat them dry with kitchen paper.
Heat 1 tablespoon oil in a cast-iron pot over medium heat.
Sear one lamb shank on both sides. Do the same with the second lamb shank.
Place the lamb shanks on a plate, cover with aluminium foil and set aside.
Sauté the carrots and onion in the leftover meat drippings until soft.
Add the garlic and sauté for another minute.
Return the shanks to the pot and season to taste with coarse salt and freshly ground pepper. Add the lamb broth.
Bake the shanks in the oven for 1 1/2 to 2 hours until the meat falls off the bone. Remove them from the oven and transfer them to a plate. Cover the shanks with foil to keep them warm.

TIPS:
- If the sauce is too thick, add a couple of tablespoons of lamb stock. If the sauce is too thin, continue to reduce the sauce over medium heat until it has reached the right consistency.
- Coat the lamb shanks with the sauce before serving.
- Serve the braised lamb shank with mashed potatoes, rice or pasta.

BARBECUED SPRING CHICKEN

Preparation time: 1 1/2 hours   Serves 4

Chicken is always a recipe for success, especially in combination with barbecue sauce. Moreover, we debone the chicken ourselves, allowing us to offer our guests a unique experience. This is a prime example of a dish that may look simple to make, but brings quite a few challenges with it when it comes to preparation. But we don't mind; on the contrary.

500 g spring chicken
100 ml barbecue sauce
50 g chicken skin crisps

Basic prep for spring chicken
10 ml white wine vinegar
30 g shallots, sliced
1 g garlic, minced
3 g salt
2 g pepper

Barbecue sauce
140 ml tomato ketchup
120 ml apple cider
120 ml soy sauce
100 g brown sugar
30 g treacle
25 ml Worcestershire sauce
20 g tomato paste
10 g salt
5 g celery seeds
5 g garlic powder
5 g cumin
5 g black pepper
2 g onion powder
2 g smoked paprika powder
0.5 g cayenne pepper

Chicken skin crisps
200 g chicken skin
20 g chicken seasoning
5 g salt
500 ml water
150 g tapioca flour

METHOD

For the barbecue sauce:
Whisk all the ingredients together in a small saucepan. Bring to a boil over medium heat, stirring regularly so the sugar dissolves nicely and the sauce doesn't burn. Simmer for 15 mins. Remove the pan from heat as soon as the sauce has reduced to the right consistency and cover. Let the sauce cool to room temperature; this should take about 30 minutes. Transfer the sauce to an airtight container. You can store this sauce in the refrigerator for up to 3 weeks.

For the chicken skin crisps:
Put all the ingredients except for the tapioca flour in a pan and cook for 30 minutes. Transfer everything to a blender and add the tapioca flour. Blend until smooth. Spoon the mixture to a pan and bring to a boil. Keep stirring constantly until you end up with a sticky mixture. Preheat the oven to 140 °C. Spread the mixture out over a silicon baking tray and cover with a second tray. Bake the crisps in the oven for 30 to 40 minutes until nice and crispy.

For the spring chicken:
Debone the chicken and marinate the meat in the vinegar, the shallots and the garlic. Add salt and pepper and leave to rest for about 20 minutes. Grill each side of the chicken for 3 minutes. Coat with barbecue sauce. Grill the chicken once more, for 2 minutes this time. Coat once again with the barbecue sauce. Serve the barbecued spring chicken with the chicken skin crisps.

AUBERGINE ALLA PARMIGIANA

Preparation time: 2 hours   Serves 4

Just like Marcelo, I love Italian cuisine. In fact, you can easily tempt me with any kind of combination of Parmesan, oil, tomato and vinegar. The challenge in this recipe was finding different cutting methods so I could play around with the aubergine's texture. I sautéed the aubergines and coated them with Parmesan cheese to give them that lovely crispy texture.

sautéed aubergines
80 g boiled aubergine-tomato fondue
30 ml tomato dressing

Tomato dressing
80 g cherry tomatoes
20 g Parmesan cheese, grated
10 g basil, finely chopped
30 g parsley, finely chopped
20 ml olive oil
20 ml white balsamic vinegar

Aubergine-tomato fondue
1 aubergine
10 ml olive oil
100 g prepared tomato fondue (p. 153)
1 g salt
1 g pepper

Sautéed aubergines
2 aubergines
30 ml olive oil
2 g salt
1 g pepper
50 g Parmesan cheese, grated

METHOD

For the tomato dressing:
Quarter the tomatoes and add the Parmesan cheese, basil, parsley, olive oil and vinegar to the tomatoes.
Season to taste with a pinch of salt if needed.

For the aubergine-tomato fondue:
Dice the aubergine into small cubes.
Sauté the diced aubergine in a pan with olive oil until cooked through. Transfer to a saucepan and add the tomato fondue. Add salt and pepper to taste.

For the sautéed aubergines:
Preheat the oven to 180 °C.
Slice the aubergines lengthways into thin strips (aim for strips about 0.5 cm thick) and arrange them on a baking tray. Add olive oil, salt, pepper, garlic and Parmesan. Bake them for 10 to 15 minutes in the oven until golden brown.

Spoon the aubergine-tomato fondue on the plate. Place the aubergine slices on top. Finish by drizzling with tomato dressing.

FISH AND CHIPS WITH TARAMA

〰️ Preparation time: 2 hours   👤 Serves 4

The inspiration for this fish and chips recipe comes from the visionary chef Heston Blumenthal and his unique molecular approach to cooking. I was so incredibly proud when I finally succeeded in making my own mouth-watering version of this traditional classic.

1 red gurnard (400 to 600 g)	Tarama	Parsley butter
50 g parsley butter	250 ml maize oil	20 g parsley, finely chopped
100 g flour	70 g white onions, finely chopped	1 g salt
60 g egg yolk	70 g cod roe (ask at your local fishmonger)	1 g black pepper
20 ml water	130 ml water	1 g garlic, minced
100 g panko	75 g panko	50 g soft butter
1 hard potato or 40 g chips	2 g salt	
1 litre oil for deep frying	10 ml lemon juice	
40 g tarama	1 g sumac	
lemon juice (optional)		

METHOD

For the tarama:
Put a small pan with a bit of maize oil over heat and sauté the minced onions over medium heat. Make sure they turn soft but never cook completely through. Combine all the ingredients except for the sumac in a blender. Blend the ingredients until smooth. Slowly add the maize oil to your mixture and blend to a nice, creamy consistency (like hummus). Garnish the tarama with sumac.

For the parsley butter:
Combine all the ingredients except for the butter and grind them with a mortar and pestle. Add the butter to the mixture and mix well.

Clean the fish thoroughly. Remove the bones, but leave the tail on, or ask your local fishmonger for advice. Put slices of parsley butter between the fish and roll the filets up tightly in cling film. Steam the fish for five minutes before chilling the fish rolls in the refrigerator for 5 hours until firm. Remove the film and coat the fish à l'anglaise in flour, then egg yolk, water and panko. Deep-fry the fish for 3 to 4 minutes at 180 °C until golden brown.

For the potato chips:
Clean the potato and slice into thin slices using a mandolin slicer. Wash the slices and pat them dry with kitchen paper. Deep-fry the slices at 160 °C until golden brown and add salt to taste.

Arrange the fried fish on your plate, spoon a dollop of tarama next to it and drizzle the chips with lemon juice if desired.

GRANDMA'S MEATLOAF WITH MASHED POTATOES

△△△ Preparation time: 1 hour   👤 Serves 4

Belgians love comfort food. Meatloaf however, takes time and love: not only should your meat be of exceptional quality, but you need to make your own stuffing (with leek, shallots and herbs) and mashed potatoes by hand. In my opinion, if you don't make everything fresh, this dish loses its unique flavour and value. This meatloaf was our bestselling dish until it eventually disappeared from the menu. Who knows, maybe I'll make a refined 2.0 version of this classic sometime soon.

700 g meatloaf
100 g pork gravy
400 g mashed potatoes

Meatloaf
30 ml olive oil
100 g leek, finely chopped
1 shallot, finely chopped
0.5 g garlic, minced
500 g mixed minced meat
10 g parsley blend
4 g Thai red chilli
1 egg
6 drops Tabasco sauce
25 g Dijon mustard
7 g curry powder
30 ml tomato ketchup
25 g panko
5 g salt

Pork gravy
80 g butter
120 g shallots
2 g garlic, sliced
100 g bacon
1 litre reduced pork broth
3 g thyme
4 g sage
40 g wholegrain mustard
4 ml lemon juice

Mashed potatoes
600 g peeled potatoes
100 ml milk
100 g butter
6 g salt
2 g pepper

METHOD

For the meatloaf:
Preheat the oven to 180 °C.
Put a pan over medium-high heat and add the olive oil together with the finely chopped leek, the shallots and the garlic.
Sauté for 10 minutes until the vegetables are softened. Remove the pan from heat and set aside to cool.
Combine all the remaining meatloaf ingredients in a bowl, mix well and add the cooled vegetables.
Mix and knead into an oval shape.
Place the meatloaf on a baking tray lined with baking parchment and bake for 25 minutes in the oven.

For the pork gravy:
Heat a small saucepan and add 40 grams butter. As soon as the butter has melted, add the shallots.
After 5 minutes, add the sliced garlic.
Continue to cook until everything is slightly caramelised and then remove the shallots and the garlic from the pan.
Return the pan to the heat and add the other half of the butter, followed by the bacon. Fry the bacon until nice and golden brown.
Heat the reduced pork broth to 80 °C.
Add the sshallots, the garlic and the slightly caramelised meat to the reduced broth. Cover and infuse for 20 minutes.
Add the thyme and infuse for another 10 minutes.
Add the sage and infuse for 5 more minutes.
Strain the liquid through a fine-mesh sieve.
Add the wholegrain mustard and the lemon juice and beat the mixture to an emulsion with a spatula.

For the mashed potatoes:
Boil the peeled potatoes until tender in a pot of salted water, and then pass them through the potato ricer.
Add the milk and the butter and mix with a hand mixer until all the ingredients are blended together nicely. Please note: you may need more milk and butter, depending on the type of potato you're using.
Add salt and pepper to taste.

Serve the meatloaf with a couple of spoonfuls of mashed potatoes. Drizzle a spoonful of pork gravy over the top and serve the remaining gravy in a small pitcher.

OSSOBUCO GIOUVETSI

Preparation time: 1 1/2 hours   Serves 4-6

Giouvetsi is a typically Greek dish made from chicken, lamb, beef or even seafood, depending on personal preferences and regional tastes. It is accompanied by a hearty tomato sauce and Greek kritharaki pasta. I treasure the fond memories I have of this dish that my former mentor and I would savour immensely together. Every time I make ossobuco giouvetsi, I think of him.

100 ml olive oil
1 kg ossobuco
2 medium-sized red onions, finely chopped
2 carrots, in slices of approx. 1 cm
2 tablespoons tomato paste
1 glass red wine
300 g tomatoes, finely chopped
2 red sweet peppers, quartered
1 teaspoon sugar
1 cinnamon stick
3 g pepper
10 g salt
500 g Greek pasta (kritharaki or manestra)
200 g Greek cheese (kefalotyri or feta), grated

METHOD

Heat half a cup of olive oil in a cast-iron pot, add the ossobuco and sear the meat on both sides until crispy.
Remove the meat from the pan and add the onions and carrots. Sauté over low-medium heat for 5 minutes.
Stir in the tomato paste and sauté the vegetable mixture for another minute before adding the red wine.
Add the ossobuco and wait until the wine has evaporated.
Then add the chopped tomatoes, the red sweet peppers, the sugar, the cinnamon stick and finally a generous pinch of salt and pepper.
Add enough water to submerge the meat.
Lower the heat, cover the pan and simmer for 45 minutes until the meat is soft and cooked through. Stir regularly and add water if the sauce gets too dry.
Meanwhile, heat a second pan and add 3 tablespoons olive oil together with the pasta.
Add boiling water and cook for 8 minutes.
Strain the pasta through a sieve and freshen it up with cold water.
Remove the meat from the pan, let it rest for a moment; meanwhile, add the drained pasta to the sauce and cook for another 2 minutes.
Transfer the meat back to the pan with the pasta and turn off the heat.

After 10 minutes, garnish with the grated Greek cheese.
Serve in a deep plate.

SEAFOOD WITH TOMATO SAUCE

〰️ Preparation time: 1 hour   👤 Serves 4

This recipe is a perfect marriage between North Sea cuisine and Italian culinary traditions. On the one hand, you have the fresh mussels, scallops, clams and razor clams. On the other hand, the tomato sauce and the many herbs remind us of the warm Mediterranean.

2 scallops
100 g mussels
80 g razor clams
60 g clams
10 ml olive oil
10 g garlic, minced

60 ml white wine
20 g thyme
2 g salt
1 g pepper
200 g prepared tomato fondue (p. 153)

METHOD

Rinse all the shellfish multiple times in cold, salted water.
Add the olive oil and the garlic to a pan and fry the scallops on one side for two minutes to a nice golden-brown colour.
Then add the mussels, razor clams and clams and fry for another 2 minutes.
Add the white wine and the thyme and continue to cook until all the alcohol has evaporated.

Add salt and pepper to taste.
Add the tomato fondue to your shellfish.
Cook for another 5 minutes, finish with salt, pepper and a dash of olive oil.
Serve in a deep plate.

Serving tip:
Use a bit of coriander for an exotic touch and serve with pasta.

FROM PICTURESQUE ZEELAND
TO BUSTLING GHENT

M I was the first to leave Pure C, and I remember how sometimes I had the nerve to call Eric in the mornings just to tease him. Because by the time I rolled out of bed, he would have been working for several hours. And then I would tell him how life away from Pure C was pure paradise in comparison. And yet I returned to Pure C. Syrco offered me a job on his research and development team on the condition that I would take on one weekend service per week. It was an arrangement that suited me just fine. Until Dominik called that life into question and asked me outright whether I wanted my own restaurant. I wasn't interested. I was happy because I could vent all my creativity into developing dishes and tastings for Pure C. Meanwhile, Dominik saw the opportunity to start a restaurant in Ghent and bought a building lot. He was convinced of my talent, and with his years of experience as an entrepreneur, the move towards opening a restaurant seemed to him the only logical next step. When I think about this rationally now, you could almost say that he brainwashed me to some extent – in the best possible way, let me add. He took care of the financial, administrative, and legal side and maintained the local network so I could focus entirely on cooking. He was the backbone; I was the performer. Although the idea of having my own restaurant appealed to me, I was instantly overcome by a crushing feeling of responsibility. Dominik managed to reduce that stress by setting a time framework for the project. I would have two years to prepare before the restaurant would open its doors. In practice, little came of the promised two years. Suddenly, those two years became six months, and I had to be ready by then. Thanks to Eric, for the most part, I was. I remember hesitatingly approaching Eric and asking him to participate in the story as my sous-chef. To him, it seemed like the most natural thing in the world. He looked at me, shrugged, and said: 'Okay, let's do it!'.

E I had already visited Ghent three times together with Eleni before Marcelo asked me to join him. And because I was utterly enamoured with the city, I didn't have to think long about my answer. Zeeland is a beautiful region, but it's sadly a bit of a backwater. I love Ghent's historical city centre. The city is a vibrant, bustling melting pot of shops, restaurants, bars, squares, and parks. I could spend hours getting lost wandering the streets together with Eleni. My daughter Athina also loves it here. Moreover, Western Europe is a fine spot to discover the rest of the world. As a former island resident, I could certainly appreciate that ability to move around.

From construction site to starry sky

E I remember rigging the electricity at three o'clock in the morning at OAK the night before the opening – together with Dominik's father, who has sadly enough passed away. We called on family and friends to lend a helping hand. Eleni and Dominik ran the service during the opening weeks because we had no staff. Eleni did so with slightly more success than Dominik, who spent hours chatting at tables, putting Marcelo and me in a tight spot when it came to getting dishes out on time.

M Eric was my anchor during those first few weeks at OAK in October 2014. For two years, we ran OAK's kitchen together by ourselves. This is a challenge in a space measuring barely two square metres, especially when you spend an average of 12 hours a day there together. There was just no escaping each other. Three years later, in the autumn of 2017, Michelin rewarded our hard work with a star. That was an ecstatic moment. Dominik's father was still alive back then, and Eric was still my right-hand man at the restaurant. As I see it, that was the day we were awarded the title of family.

Meanwhile, we could also sense that our guests' expectations were rising. We were receiving more and more comments that the street in which our restaurant was located wasn't the nicest and that our restaurant was very limited in terms of space. Still, OAK's setting and philosophy felt right and natural to me. I never intended to run a large restaurant, let alone two. The danger in stars, scores, and lists is that you start to compare your restaurant to others, when in fact you're being rewarded for your uniqueness. It is important not to lose your soul in all those rankings. I always advise chefs never to cook according to the opinion of others but to create their own path. The goal is to develop your cooking to become a reflection of yourself, not to copy the success of others. Otherwise, chances are you'll become a commodity.

TOMATO BURRATA WITH MUHAMMARA

Preparation time: 1 hour   Serves 4

This recipe is a blend of my Greek love for tomatoes and my traineeship with Yotam Ottolenghi. Marcelo had also briefly worked with him and he arranged a traineeship for me prior to the opening of DOOR73. Greek cuisine, with its distinctive flavours and spices has a lot in common with Middle-Eastern cuisine. In fact, this recipe combines the best of Italy (the burrata), Greece (the tomatoes), and the Middle East (the muhammara).

50 g cherry tomatoes
10 ml olive oil
3 g salt
1 g pepper
2 g thyme
125 g burrata
1 g lemon zest
50 g muhammara
80 ml tomato juice
20 ml chive oil
10 g dried tomato powder

Muhammara
150 g cooked red sweet peppers
85 g Parmesan cheese
25 g pine nuts
30 g pistachios
40 ml olive oil
18 ml Cabernet Sauvignon vinegar
5 g garlic
20 g parsley
8 g smoked paprika powder
6 g salt
1 g chilli powder
1 g ground cumin

Tomato juice
300 g sweet tomatoes
30 ml white balsamic vinegar
5 g salt

Chive oil
900 ml maize oil
300 g chives

METHOD

For the muhammara:
Grill the peppers in an oven preheated to 180 °C until soft. Peel off the skin, remove the seeds and put them in a blender together with the other ingredients. Blend the ingredients into a smooth paste.

For the tomato juice:
Press the sweet tomatoes through a fine-mesh sieve and put them in the blender. Add salt and vinegar to taste.

For the chive oil:
Heat the maize oil in a small saucepan to 70 °C. Finely chop the chives in a blender and add them to the oil. Deep-fry the chives very briefly before removing the pan from heat. Pour the oil mixture through a sieve. The chive oil will keep for up to 1 month after it has cooled.

Slice the cherry tomatoes in half and spread them out on a baking tray. Season with the olive oil, the salt, the pepper and the thyme and bake for 30 minutes in an oven at 150 °C until they're halfway dry. Season the burrata to taste with olive oil, salt, pepper and a bit of lemon zest. Start with a spoonful of muhammara on a plate and arrange the burrata on top. Arrange the semi-dried cherry tomatoes around the burrata and garnish with the tomato juice, chive oil and dried tomato powder.

FISH PIE

⌁ Preparation time: 1 hour   👤 Serves 4

This pie is based on a typical English-style pie, except I use shrimp, calamari and béchamel sauce in addition to the traditional cod. That's how I've given this classic a personal twist.

300 ml prepared tomato fondue (p. 153)
4 jumbo shrimp (size 6-9)
200 g cod
50 g calamari
100 ml béchamel sauce
1 sheet of puff pastry (with a diameter of 60 cm)
20 g egg yolk
10 ml milk

Béchamel sauce
30 g butter
20 g flour
200 ml milk
4 g salt
0.5 g pepper
1 g garlic powder
10 g coriander, finely chopped
10 g parsley, finely chopped
10 g dill, finely chopped

METHOD

For the béchamel sauce:
Place a small saucepan over medium-high heat, add the butter and let it melt.
Add the flour and cook for 2-3 minutes.
Then add the milk and cook the sauce for 5 to 10 minutes until the milk thickens.
Add salt, pepper, garlic and finally the finely-chopped herbs.

Preheat the oven to 200 °C.
Spoon the tomato fondue into a cast-iron pan. Add the cleaned shrimp and pieces of fish.
Pour the béchamel sauce over the top. Cover the pie with the puff pastry, and prick holes into the pastry with a fork.
Coat the puff pastry with a layer of beaten egg yolk (with a bit of milk mixed in) and bake for 20 to 25 minutes in the oven until the pie is cooked through.
Serve warm.

GREEN ASPARAGUS WITH CRUSTY SOURDOUGH BREAD AND SPICY TOMATO SAUCE

Preparation time: 30 minutes   Serves 2-4

This is a hearty vegetable-based meal that we give an added richness with the pecorino and herbed buckwheat. The fresh, grilled asparagus immediately lend a bright, spring touch to the dish, with a spicy kick from the tomato sauce.

100 g green asparagus
1 slice sourdough bread
10 ml olive oil
2 g salt
1 g garlic, grated
1 g pepper
50 g spicy tomato sauce
10 g buckwheat blend
20 g pecorino cheese, grated

Spicy tomato sauce
50 ml olive oil
50 g yellow onion, finely chopped
15 g garlic, minced
3 San Marzano tomatoes, diced
20 g red chilli flakes, crushed to a fine powder
3 g salt
1 g freshly ground black pepper
2 ml Tabasco sauce (optional)

Buckwheat blend
50 g buckwheat
10 g poppy seeds
10 g black sesame seeds
5 g Maldon salt

METHOD

Blanch the asparagus for 2 minutes in salted water and submerge them in iced water immediately afterwards. Set aside.

For the spicy tomato sauce:
Put the olive oil, onion and garlic in a medium-sized pan and sauté until soft. Add the tomatoes to the mixture together with the juice. Use a wooden spoon or a potato masher to carefully break up the tomatoes as they heat up. Let the sauce simmer and add the red chilli flakes. Simmer over low heat for about 30 minutes until the sauce has the desired consistency. Finish the sauce by adding salt and pepper to taste. Season with Tabasco if desired.

For the buckwheat blend:
Bake the buckwheat for 10 mins. in an oven preheated to 160 °C and combine with the other ingredients.

Slice the sourdough bread into thin slices and sprinkle olive oil, salt and grated garlic over the top. Grill the slices in an oven preheated to 180 °C until crispy. Grill the asparagus until golden brown and season with salt and pepper to taste. Arrange them on the bread and serve a dollop of the spicy tomato sauce next to it. Garnish with the buckwheat blend and some grated pecorino cheese.

BUTTER BEANS WITH SAMBAL

Preparation time: 1 hour   Serves 2-4

One of our Asian trainees gave me the idea to make a spicy vegetarian dish — he had the regular habit of preparing spicy vegetables with noodles for his own meals. Butter beans with sambal is the perfect savoury side dish to accompany an Asian-inspired fish dish. Give it a try!

200 g butter beans
20 ml olive oil
1 g salt
80 g sambal
lemon zest
20 g spring onions, finely chopped
50 g spiced peanuts
20 g Thai red chilli, finely chopped
60 ml ponzu-soy dressing

Sambal
5 white onions
5 red onions
25 g ginger
80 g lemongrass
7 g coriander seeds
25 g red chilli peppers
3 g lime leaf
30 g garlic
200 ml maize oil
300 g tomato paste

Spiced peanuts
75 g red curry paste
200 g spiced peanuts, halved
200 ml water
150 g brown sugar

Ponzu-soy dressing
20 ml ponzu
10 ml soy sauce
20 ml sushi vinegar
10 ml yuzu juice
10 ml olive oil

METHOD

For the sambal:
Preheat the oven to 160 °C. Peel and finely chop the onions. Put the onions in baking dish and cover with a lid or another dish. Place the dish in the oven and bake the onions for 25 minutes. Chop the ginger and lemongrass into very fine pieces. Grind the coriander seeds down to a fine powder. Mix all the spices, the finely chopped ginger and lemon grass and maize oil to a fine puree. Put a pan on the heat and add the spiced puree; sauté for 5 minutes. Add the chopped onions, stir well and cook for 20 minutes. Stir regularly. After 20 minutes, add the tomato paste and leave the mixture to simmer for 3 1/2 hours. Allow the sambal to cool before use. You can store the sambal in the refrigerator for up to two weeks.

For the spiced peanuts:
Combine all the ingredients in a medium-sized saucepan and simmer for about 10 minutes until the spiced peanuts are soft. Cover with foil and let the mixture cool for 6 hours. Preheat the oven to 140 °C. Take the peanuts out of the pan with a slotted spoon and spread them out over a baking tray. Bake them in the oven for 30 minutes or until crunchy, stirring every 10 minutes. Let the spiced peanuts cool before use.

For the ponzu-soy dressing:
Combine all the ingredients into a dressing.

For the butter beans:
Boil the beans in salted water for 3 to 4 minutes.
Submerge them in iced water and then sauté in a pan with olive oil.

Combine the beans with the sambal, garnish with salt and the lime zest.
Arrange the beans on a plate, add the spring onions, the spiced peanuts and Thai chillies; then drizzle the ponzu-soy dressing over the top.

Serving tip:
Add some finely chopped mint or watercress for a refreshing touch.

YOUNG CAULIFLOWER WITH TAHINI DRESSING, SALSA, MISO AND DUKKHA

Preparation time: 1 hour   Serves 4

DOOR73 wants to be accessible to everyone. That's why we also pull out all the stops with several vegetable-based dishes, such as this cauliflower dish. We used to serve the entire cauliflower, but this family-sized portion proved to be too much of a good thing for most of our guests. Our sauce (based on tahini, salsa, miso and dukkha), however, has remained the same by popular demand. Dip at your own risk!

1 young cauliflower (approx. 500 g)
200 g butter
50 ml miso glaze
80 ml tahini dressing
60 g salsa verde
30 g dukkha
10 g mint
10 g parsley

Tahini dressing
105 g tahini
210 g Greek-style yoghurt
1 g garlic
20 ml lemon juice
4 g salt
50 to 80 ml water

Salsa verde
60 g fresh coriander
90 g parsley
2 g garlic
1 green pepper

225 ml olive oil
20 ml Cabernet Sauvignon vinegar

Miso glaze
200 g brown miso
600 ml sweet soy sauce

Dukkha
50 g cumin seeds
130 g coriander seeds
120 g hazelnuts
120 g sesame seeds

METHOD

For the tahini dressing:
Combine all the ingredients and add an equal part water to make a creamy dressing.

For the salsa verde:
Mix all the ingredients in a blender to until creamy.

For the miso glaze:
Mix the ingredients.

For the dukkha:
Bake the cumin and coriander seeds for 5 minutes in an oven preheated to 170 °C until golden brown. Lower the oven temperature to 160 °C and bake the hazelnuts for 15 minutes. Stir them around every 5 minutes. Finely chop the hazelnuts. Put the cumin and coriander seeds in a mortar and grind until half the seeds are crushed. Then spoon them into a bowl and add the sesame seeds and chopped hazelnuts.

Take a saucepan and cook the cauliflower in salted water for 3 to 4 minutes. Transfer the cauliflower to a bowl. Raise the oven temperature to 190 °C and melt the butter in a small saucepan. Coat the cauliflower with the butter or olive oil and bake for 7 minutes in the oven. Repeat this process three more times so the cauliflower turns golden-brown and cooks through to the middle. Coat the cauliflower with the miso glaze and arrange on a plate. Garnish with the tahini dressing, the salsa verde, and finally the dukkha, mint and parsley.

GRILLED SEA BASS WITH CAPER DRESSING AND PARSLEY OIL

Preparation time: 1 hour   Serves 4

Grilled sea bass is one of our most classic and popular dishes on the menu, but it's also highly popular in Greece, especially in the coastal areas and on the islands. Sea fennel, better known as kritamo in Greece, is often used in salads, as seasoning for fish dishes or as a garnish. I mostly appreciate its unique flavour and the way sea fennel manages to add depth to dishes.

1 sea bass (approx. 400 to 600 g)
3 g salt
60 ml caper dressing
100 ml parsley oil
20 g lemon
30 g kritamo
20 g fennel fronds

Caper dressing
100 g capers
120 g pickles
80 g shallots
10 ml Tabasco sauce
20 ml Worcestershire sauce
2.5 g salt
40 g anchovies
50 g Parmesan cheese

Parsley oil
300 g parsley
900 ml maize oil

METHOD

For the caper dressing:
Combine all the ingredients.

For the parsley oil:
Mix the ingredients in a blender, then bring to a boil in a pan over medium heat. Strain the liquid through a fine-mesh sieve.

Fillet the fish, sprinkle with salt and grill for 2 minutes on each side.
Arrange the sea bass on a platter, add the dressing, the oil and a couple of lemon slices.
Garnish with the kritamo and fennel fronds.

POACHED COD IN RED CURRY SAUCE

Preparation time: 45 minutes   Serves 4

When I started at Pure C some eleven years ago, the only sauce I was familiar with was tomato sauce. Chef Syrco Bakker broadened my horizons by introducing me to a whole new world of Asian-inspired sauces. Marcelo in turn took me to the finer Asian restaurants, where I was spontaneously inspired to create my own version of a curry.

2 tablespoons olive oil
100 g white onions
70 g ginger, finely chopped
3 garlic cloves, minced
1 Thai red chilli pepper
2 kaffir lime leaves
80 g lemongrass, finely ground
45 g Thai red curry paste
1 can coconut milk

1 tablespoon curry powder
200 ml water
1 tablespoon fish sauce
1 tablespoon brown sugar
5 g salt
300 g cod
30 ml lime juice
30 g coriander, finely chopped

METHOD

Heat the oil in a large pan over medium heat.
Add the onion, ginger, garlic, chillies, kaffir lime leaves and lemongrass and sauté until golden brown for about 5 minutes.
Then add the curry paste, coconut milk, curry powder and water and simmer for 20 minutes.
Finish the sauce with fish sauce and sugar, taste the sauce and add salt if needed.
Simmer the cod for 5 minutes in the pan until cooked through.
Arrange the fish on a plate.
Strain the sauce through a fine-mesh sieve, drizzle the sauce over the fish and garnish before serving with the lime juice and finely chopped coriander.

HITTING THE ROAD WITH A BACKPACK FULL OF INSPIRATION

E OAK's status and Marcelo's popularity made me feel like the training wheels had come off far too quickly at DOOR73. Some people thought they were making reservations for OAK's brasserie, while the kitchen, team, and philosophy embodied something different. When the first critic had a lukewarm reaction to our sharing formula, I felt rotten for weeks. Then, one day, a restaurant critic who did understand what we were trying to do came in. When not much later we were crowned Gastro-Bistro of the year by Gault&Millau, it did wonders for me and my staff in terms of confidence. In hindsight, I'm even convinced that that first poor review encouraged me to question myself and bring out the best in me. Were my dishes getting the refinement and depth they deserved? Was my cooking as focused as I'd initially planned? That drive for constant improvement is something that's simply in me; I don't need any guides or lists to help me. My most important focus is the guests and ensuring they're satisfied. That's why we've invested a lot of time and energy in clarifying our vision of a restaurant based on the concept of sharing. You're not meant to combine dishes to create your own taste experience, because then the dishes would lose their cohesion. The idea is that you order several dishes – more than the classic first course, main course and dessert – so you have a constant supply of food. I always make sure that each of our dishes is unique to provide food for thought and conversation. Often you can't place them under the umbrella one particular cuisine. They are not simply Greek or Mediterranean. I often use an oil, chilli peppers, tapioca, or fermented beans from Brazil, my clams are prepared Taiwanese style, and chances are you won't find mackerel with sambal on any other menu. Still, I always ensure that my products and preparations remain recognisable so our guests can orient themselves. But an unknown ingredient that adds flavour, spice, or acidity to a dish: why not?

DOOR73's signature

E I remember Marcelo was in South Korea shooting footage for a television programme when DOOR73 opened. Which was insane, in particular because I felt like I was suddenly thrown into the deep end. My initial idea was to simplify OAK's essence and add my vision of delicious food. My reasoning was relatively basic in that respect. As a chef, you need to ensure quality and consistency above everything else. Every guest should be served the same quality at any time. And then you can get creative in the décor of your business, your choice of music... Gastronomy is still far too often likened to a formal restaurant that exudes luxury or where the menu is considered incomplete without the obligatory caviar. It really doesn't have to be that way. You can focus on becoming accessible while maintaining that characteristic eye for detail and service. I personally love a typical summer atmosphere. And because the chances of soaking up some sunshine in Belgium are few and far between as opposed to, let's say, Crete, we tried to evoke that light, outdoorsy feeling at DOOR73 by integrating skylights in the restaurant. It makes me feel like I am cooking out on the patio instead of indoors, a happy, free feeling I pass on to the guests.

E DOOR73 has been open for four years now. We're now entering our fifth year, and I consider this a phase where I find more time to develop myself. And by that, I mean the creativity in the kitchen and the dynamic between our staff members. In terms of cooking style, I focus on pure products in recognisable preparations, without tweezers, flowers, or obscure jellies. I want to excel in the basics, so I'm the type of cook who makes his dough from scratch and spends hours working on a dip until it has just the right consistency. In fact, I make dishes that you would probably want to eat at home but that require far too much work to create that same finishing touch. DOOR73 has also changed me as a person over the years. I am rather quiet by nature. You could hardly call me a born leader, which is unfortunate in a sense because how you run your restaurant is crucial to how your business is organised. I tend to let the stress build up in me until my pot boils over. Everyone knows that you're allowed to make mistakes in my kitchen, just not the same one over and over again. I have had to learn to tame my inner hurricane, not just for the people around me but for myself as well. The biggest challenge for any chef or anyone owning a catering business is to build up a solid team. I put a lot of my time and energy into doing so. Managing my team was a nightmare during the start-up phase. I didn't know how to react when someone was upset, and I was always sticking my nose into someone else's pots. You simply forget the human aspect in the stressful throes of service; you must give your staff the chance to grow. Now I know that you can challenge someone to get creative by giving that person time to develop a new vegetarian dish, for example.

M I know that it may sound a bit strange coming from me, but DOOR73 is one of my favourite restaurants. The relaxed atmosphere, the unusual music, the delicious cocktails, and world-inspired comfort food all work for me. Nowadays, I feel more like a guest than a business partner whenever I visit. I don't feel any need to know what's happening at DOOR73. If I come across something interesting, I'll share it with Eric, and he knows that he can always come to me if he has any questions. I help him think up ideas, but Eric makes the decisions and determines what ends up on the menu. Still, I don't wear kid gloves when he has questions or asks for feedback. I am convinced that every day presents an opportunity to be even better than the day before. Anyone who gets complacent ends up in the comfort zone and stagnates. I fear and hate the comfort zone. Sometimes you're stuck perfecting a certain preparation, and that feeling of being stuck starts to become your reality in a literal sense. Suddenly your entire menu, your staff and even your restaurant's appearance feels like an assembly line and that gnaws at you. Because, as a creative chef, you're always looking for something new, the next step. I have always felt that hunger for more.

CHIPOTLE PORTOBELLO

Preparation time: 2 hours   Serves 4-6

Portobello mushrooms are famous for their meaty texture and robust flavour, making them an excellent ingredient for our vegetarian dishes. Their earthy flavour pairs perfectly with a rich oil or dressing, as is the case here.

8 medium-sized portobellos (approx. 650 g)
10 cloves garlic
150 g white onions
15 g red chilli peppers
30 g cumin seeds, coarsely ground
10 g coriander seeds, coarsely ground
60 g tomato paste
300 ml olive oil
1 tablespoon salt flakes
60 g yoghurt dressing
20 ml spring onion oil

Yoghurt dressing
80 g Greek-style yoghurt
20 ml water
20 ml lemon juice
10 ml white wine vinegar
5 g cumin powder
2 g salt
2 g pepper

Spring onion oil
300 g spring onions
900 ml maize oil

METHOD

For the yoghurt dressing:
Combine all the ingredients and taste to see if it needs more salt or pepper.

For the spring onion oil:
Blend the onions with the oil with a stick blender. Heat the mixture in a saucepan before straining it through a sieve.

Preheat the oven to 150 °C.
Combine all the ingredients (except for the yoghurt dressing and the spring onion oil) in an ovenproof saucepan with a lid. Arrange the portobello mushrooms in the pan with the rounded side facing up and cover them with a piece of parchment paper. Cover the pan with a lid and bake in the oven for 1 hour. Turn the portobello mushrooms over, cover once more with parchment paper and bake for a further 20 minutes in the oven. Remove the pan from the oven once the portobello mushrooms are soft but not falling apart. Transfer the portobello mushrooms to a cutting board with a pair of tongs; slice them down the middle and set aside. Use a spoon to remove the onion, garlic and chilli pepper. Spoon the remaining mixture into a blender and blend into a smooth paste. Return the blended mixture to the pan together with the portobello halves and place over medium heat. Reduce everything for about 5 minutes to allow the flavours to blend together nicely. Arrange the portobello mushrooms on a plate with a scoop of onion mixture next to them. Finish with the yoghurt dressing and the spring onion oil.

CHICKEN TIKKA MASALA KATAIFI

~~~ Preparation time: 2 hours   👤 Serves 2-4

Kataifi means (literally translated from Greek) 'spun dough', although it is commonly just as often referred to as shredded dough. Chicken tikka masala is a heart-warming dish that involves marinating tender chicken pieces in spicy spices and yoghurt and serving them in a creamy tomato sauce. A dish I enjoy time and time again. With the gossamer-thin kataifi, I add my own touch and crispy texture to this Indian classic.

2 corn-fed chicken breasts (approx. 300 g)
5 g salt
2 g pepper
30 g butter
100 g kataifi dough
100 g tikka masala
50 g yoghurt dressing
20 ml chive oil

Tikka masala
70 ml maize oil
150 g white onions, finely chopped
2 garlic cloves, minced
20 g ginger, finely chopped
1 Thai red chilli pepper, finely chopped, seeds included
10 g brown sugar
100 g tomato paste
4 g coriander powder
10 g cumin powder
7 g garam masala
4 g smoked paprika powder
2 g salt

Yoghurt dressing
80 g Greek-style yoghurt
20 ml water
20 ml lemon juice
10 ml white wine vinegar
5 g cumin powder
2 g salt
2 g pepper

Chive oil
300 g chives
900 ml maize oil

METHOD

For the chive oil:
Heat the maize oil in a small saucepan to 70 °C.
Finely chop the chives in a blender and add them to the oil. Deep-fry the chives very briefly before removing the pan from heat.
Pour the oil mixture through a sieve. The chive oil will keep for up to 1 month after it has cooled.

For the yoghurt dressing:
Combine all the ingredients and taste to see if it needs more salt or pepper.

For the tikka masala:
Add the maize oil to a pan, followed by the onions and the garlic.
Sauté the ingredients for 3 minutes before adding the ginger and chilli pepper.
Sauté for another 5 minutes and then add the sugar and the tomato paste, together with all the spices.
Lower the heat and cook for 30 minutes to a dry paste with all the moisture removed.
Combine the mixture into a smooth cream and season the tikka masala with salt.

Place both chicken breasts next to each other on the workbench and sprinkle salt and pepper over the top.
Stack them on top of each other and roll in cling film.
Steam the chicken breasts for 40 minutes at 65 °C, then leave the meat to cool in the refrigerator.
Remove the cling film from the chicken and fry the chicken breasts in a pan until golden brown in colour.
Preheat the oven to 180 °C.
Melt the butter.
Add the chicken to the kataifi dough, roll everything up and coat with the melted butter.
Bake for 12 to 15 minutes in the oven until the chicken turns golden brown.
Remove the chicken from the oven and leave to rest.
Compose a plate by putting a spoonful of the tikka masala, add the chicken, and finish with the yoghurt dressing and chive oil.

BRAZILIAN CURRY WITH GAMBERO ROSSO AND PIMENTA-DE-BODE CHILLI

Preparation time: 1 hour Serves 2

Marcelo and I felt it was important to introduce Brazilian flavours to DOOR 73 as well; consider it an ode to Marcelo's homeland. I try to capture the essence of the Brazilian kitchen by using spicy chillies. Brazilians love pronounced flavours.

10 ml olive oil
200 g gambero rosso (red prawns)
50 g red sweet peppers
30 g pimenta-de-bode chillies
100 ml organic palm oil sauce
20 ml organic palm oil

Organic palm oil sauce
80 ml maize oil
200 g white onions, thinly sliced
1 garlic clove, minced
20 g red chilli peppers, thinly sliced
40 ml organic palm oil
1 litre coconut milk
30 g coriander, finely chopped
3 g salt

METHOD

For the palm oil sauce:
Add the maize oil to a small pan over high heat.
Add the onions and garlic and sauté for 6 to 7 minutes until soft.
Then add the red chillies and the palm oil and cook for an additional 5 minutes.
Add the coconut milk to the mixture and simmer for about 20 minutes.
Finish with the coriander.
Let the sauce rest for another 20 minutes before straining through a sieve.
Add salt to taste.

Add a splash of olive oil to a large pan and fry the gambero rosso on both sides.
Peel the red sweet peppers and fry them for 2 minutes in another pan.
Then add the red sweet peppers and the pimenta-de-bode chillies to the pan with the gambero rosso and combine.
Serve the spicy gambero rosso first and deglaze with the palm oil sauce and a splash of palm oil.

DUCK CONFIT

Preparation time: 1 hour   **Serves 4**

My first visit to Belgium left a profound impression on me. I tasted a duck salad in Pastis, the restaurant owned by my friend Njegoš Kaličanin. I have been crazy about duck confit ever since. Duck confit is a classic French preparation where the duck is slowly cooked in its own fat to produce incredibly tender, flavourful meat. I like to keep my preparation as simple as possible because duck in itself has a distinctive flavour.

300 g duck confit
30 g cucumber, thinly sliced
30 g daikon, thinly sliced
40 g watercress
30 g mango, sliced
50 ml duck broth
5 g maceron pepper
5 g kampot pepper

Duck confit
500 g duck legs
250 ml soy sauce
100 g brown sugar
1 cinnamon stick
2 star anise
10 g black pepper

METHOD

For the duck confit:
Combine all the ingredients for the confit in a vacuum pouch and steam for 9 hours at 75 °C.
Let the confit rest in the refrigerator for 5 hours, remove the duck leg from the vacuum pouch and remove the bone.
Spoon the remaining ingredients over into a pan and heat.
Separate the broth from the other ingredients.
Reduce the broth by half, check the taste and add extra pepper if needed.

Preheat the oven to 180 °C.
First, sear the duck leg in a pan before cooking the duck for another 7 minutes in the oven.
Arrange the warm duck leg on a plate and add the cucumber, the daikon, the watercress and the mango.
Finish with the broth and add both pepper varieties.

TOMATO SALAD WITH FETA AND OREGANO OIL

Preparation time: 12 hours   Serves 4

Upon returning from a trip to Lebanon, Hannes Verniers told me about a tomato salad with incredibly intense flavours; the result of a 12-hour drying process. His story led me to consider creating a new version of a typical Greek salad. I used slow-roasted, sweet and sour tomatoes as the basis and combined them with feta, olive oil and a juice made from cucumber, celery and apple. The only downside is that you have to take into account the tomato season, which means that you can prepare this salad only three months out of each year.

1 Noire d'Antan tomato
50 g feta
2 g dried oregano
20 ml olive oil
lemon zest
pinch of salt
80 ml cucumber-celery-apple juice
10 ml oregano oil

Cucumber-celery-apple juice
250 ml apple juice
75 g cucumber
15 g sugar
25 g celery
2 g salt

Oregano oil
100 g fresh oregano
300 ml maize oil

METHOD

Put a large pot over heat. Fill the pot with water and add salt.
Preheat the oven to 55 °C.
Blanch the tomato for 7 seconds, then submerge in iced water and peel off the outer skin.
Pat the tomato dry with kitchen paper before slow-roasting the tomato in the oven for 12 hours.

For the juice:
Combine all the ingredients and strain through a sieve. Please note: this fresh, clear juice will only keep for a couple of hours.

For the oregano oil:
Blend all the ingredients, strain through a fine-mesh sieve and heat the oil in a pan. Let it cool before serving.

Combine the feta, oregano and olive oil in a bowl.
Arrange the feta in the middle of a plate, and place the tomato on top. Top with lemon zest and a pinch of salt.
Finish the dish by drizzling the green juice and the oregano oil over the tomato salad.

SHORT RIBS WITH CASHEWS AND BARBECUE SAUCE

〰️ Preparation time: 5 to 6 hours   👤 Serves 4

The inspiration for this street food dish comes from Thailand. I needed to find a use for my leftover stock of cashews and came up with a dried paste that is sadly quite time-consuming. It's also important that you brine the meat a day ahead of time. And choose fresh herbs and ribs with a bit of fat on them to prevent them from drying out too quickly.

300 g short ribs
salt
pepper
olive oil
50 ml barbecue sauce
100 g curried cashews
10 g Thai red chilli pepper, finely chopped
40 g coriander, finely chopped

Barbecue sauce
140 ml tomato ketchup
120 ml apple cider
120 ml soy sauce
100 g brown sugar
30 g treacle
25 ml Worcestershire sauce
20 g tomato paste

10 g salt
5 g celery seeds
5 g garlic powder
5 g cumin
5 g black pepper
2 g onion powder
2 g smoked paprika powder
0.5 g cayenne pepper

Curried cashews
75 g red curry paste
200 g cashews
200 ml water
150 g brown sugar

METHOD

For the barbecue sauce:
Whisk all the ingredients together in a small saucepan.
Bring to a boil over medium heat, stirring regularly so the sugar dissolves nicely and the sauce doesn't burn.
Simmer for 15 mins.
Remove the pan from heat as soon as the thickened sauce starts to simmer and cover.
Let the sauce cool to room temperature; this should take about 30 minutes.
Transfer the sauce to an airtight container. You can store this sauce in the refrigerator for up to 3 weeks.

For the curried cashews:
Combine all the ingredients in a medium-sized saucepan and simmer for about 10 minutes until the cashews are soft.
Cover with film and let the mixture cool for 6 hours.
Preheat the oven to 140 °C.
Take the cashews out of the pan with a slotted spoon and spread them out over a baking tray.
Bake them for 30 minutes until crunchy in the oven, stirring every 10 minutes.
Let the cashews cool before use.

Spoon the ribs into an aluminium container, add salt, pepper and a bit of olive oil and cover with aluminium foil.
Slow-roast the meat at 140 °C for 4 to 5 hours until soft and tender.
Drizzle the barbecue sauce over the meat, raise the heat to 180 °C and bake the ribs for 5 minutes. Repeat this step two more times.
Serve the ribs on a plate or in a bowl with the cashews, chilli and coriander.

NORTH SEA CRAB WITH BAHĀRĀT, KRITHARAKI AND XO SAUCE

〰️ Preparation time: 3 hours   👤 Serves 4

This combination is the result of my search for a paella dish that involves me serving a whole crab — nothing of the crab goes to waste; even the heads exude flavour. The claws are used for a salad, while the legs are coated with bahārāt, a distinctive spice mixture made with paprika, coriander, black pepper, cinnamon, cumin, cardamom, onion, garlic, nutmeg, cloves and cayenne pepper from the Middle East. With it, I serve kritharaki, a Greek long-grain pasta, and Marcelo's version of an XO sauce.

60 g butter
2 cloves garlic
2 sprigs thyme
1 kg North Sea crab
100 g crab claws
1/2 lemon peel
3 g salt
200 g kritharaki
60 g bahārāt paste
30 g jalapeño salsa verde
20 ml XO sauce
50 g sofrito
60 g tomato fondue
30 ml crayfish broth
100 g crab salad
40 g aioli

Bahārāt paste
60 ml olive oil
200 g white onions, finely chopped
12 g garlic, minced
5 g Thai red chilli pepper
5 g coriander seeds
20 g bahārāt spices
50 g tomato paste
1 lemon peel
salt

Jalapeño salsa verde
15 g parsley, finely chopped
15 g coriander, finely chopped
10 g jalapeño, diced into small cubes
20 g shallots, finely chopped
30 ml olive oil
1 g garlic, minced
10 ml cherry vinegar
2 ml Tabasco sauce
4 g salt

Sofrito
40 ml olive oil
50 g white onions, diced into small cubes
10 g garlic
50 g green sweet pepper
125 g tomatoes, diced into small cubes
1 g pepper
3 g salt

Tomato fondue
80 ml olive oil
150 g white onions, diced
3 slices garlic
0.5 g coriander seeds
1 clove
1/2 star anise
600 g tomato pulp (fresh or canned)
12 ml tomato ketchup
2 drops Tabasco sauce
1 g ground black pepper
10 g Tierenteyn mustard
4 ml Worcestershire sauce
1 ml cherry vinegar
8 g salt

Crayfish broth
1 kg crayfish claws
60 ml sunflower oil
2 g white onions, finely chopped
2 garlic cloves, minced
50 g celery, finely chopped
3 medium-sized carrots,
　　finely chopped
1 star anise
50 g tomato paste
2 fresh tomatoes, halved
30 ml Ricard
30 ml white port
30 ml Noilly Prat

XO sauce
100 ml rice bran oil
30 g shallots, finely chopped
30 g garlic, minced
20 g dried shrimp
15 g fresh chilli pepper
15 g Korean chilli (gochugaru) flakes
50 g crispy onions
10 ml soy sauce
10 ml oyster sauce

Crab
1 kg North Sea crab
40 g salt
5 litres water

Kritharaki
100 g kritharaki pasta
20 ml olive oil
60 g butter
30 g shallots, finely chopped
40 g sofrito
60 g tomato fondue
80 ml crayfish broth
40 g Parmesan cheese, grated
5 g salt
1 g pepper
20 g parsley, finely chopped

Aioli
50 g garlic confit
100 g egg yolk
9 ml Chardonnay vinegar
1 g fresh garlic
60 ml water
700 ml maize oil

Crab salad
100 g crab meat (from the claws)
40 g sobrasada, diced in to small cubes
20 g bahārāt paste
40 g aioli
leftover meat from the head
　　of the crab
20 ml olive oil
2 g salt
lemon zest

METHOD

For the bahārāt paste:
Pour the olive oil in a pan over medium heat. Sauté the onions and garlic in the pan until soft.
Then add the chilli peppers, the coriander seeds and the bahārāt spices and fry for 5 minutes.
Finally add the tomato paste and cook for 30 minutes over low heat until all the moisture has evaporated. Add salt to taste.

For the jalapeño salsa verde:
Combine all the ingredients to a salsa and add salt to taste.

For the sofrito:
Pour the olive oil in a medium-sized pan. Sauté the onions and garlic in the pan until soft.
Then add the sweet pepper and the tomatoes.
Fry for 15 minutes until everything is cooked through and the liquid is reduced by half.
Set aside and let the sofrito cool.
Season with salt and pepper.

For the tomato fondue:
Pour the olive oil in a medium-sized pan. Sauté the onions and garlic for 5 minutes.
Then add the coriander, the clove and the piece of star anise and cook for an additional 5 minutes.
Add the tomato pulp and leave the sauce to gently simmer over low heat for about an hour. Stir regularly to prevent the tomatoes from sticking to the bottom of the pan.
Cook the sauce until practically all the moisture has evaporated from the sauce and it has the desired consistency.
Remove the pan from heat and add the ketchup, followed by the Tabasco sauce, black pepper, mustard, Worcestershire sauce, cherry vinegar and salt.

For the crayfish broth:
Bake the crayfish for 20 mins. in an oven preheated to 180 °C.
Pour the sunflower oil in a pan. Sauté the onions and garlic in the pan until soft.
Add the celery, carrot and the star anise. Cook for another 10 minutes.
Add the tomato paste, fresh tomatoes and crayfish.
Break their claws and add enough water to submerge all the ingredients.
Simmer the mixture over low heat for 30 to 40 minutes.
Let the broth cool and strain with a sieve.
Reduce the alcohol in a separate pan until the alcohol has evaporated and add the liquid to the broth.

For the XO sauce:
Heat the oil in a small pan. Sauté the shallots and garlic in the pan until soft.
Add the shrimp and both chilli peppers and fry for 10 minutes, stirring constantly.
In the last minute, add the onions, the soy sauce and the oyster sauce and give the sauce a brisk stir.

For the crab:
Dissolve the salt in a pan containing 5 litres boiling water, add the crab and cook for 5 minutes.
Take the crab out of the pan and submerge in iced water.
Clean the head and remove the edible crab meat for the salad.
Pull the legs from the crab and do the same with the claws; break them up and remove the meat. Make sure that you preserve the shells so you can use them to garnish your dish.

For the kritharaki:
Cook the kritharaki pasta for 10 minutes in boiling water and then submerge in cold water.
Add a little bit of olive oil so the pasta does not stick together.
In a small saucepan, melt half the butter and add the finely chopped shallots.
Sauté for 2 minutes and then add the kritharaki pasta.
Cook for another minute and then add the sofrito, followed by the tomato fondue, broth and Parmesan cheese.
Combine and season to taste with salt, pepper and chopped parsley.
Stir some more butter into the pasta just before serving.

For the aioli:
Combine all the aioli ingredients except for the oil.
Slowly add the oil until you obtain a creamy mayonnaise.

For the crab salad:
Combine all the salad ingredients and season to taste with salt and lemon.

Preheat the oven to 200 °C.
Add the butter, garlic and thyme to a pan.
Increase the heat, add the crab shell, claws and legs and cook everything for a brief minute.
Then bake the mixture in the oven for 5 minutes. Set aside and add the lemon peel and salt just before serving.
Serve the kritharaki in a deep dish, arrange the crab shell on top and fill the shell with some of the bahārāt paste.
Arrange the crab craws on a second plate and drizzle the jalapeño salsa verde and XO sauce over the top.
Serve with the aioli and the crab salad.

HAMACHI KAMA WITH GRILLED KIMCHI

Preparation time: 1 hour   Serves 2-4

Hamachi kama, also known as yellowtail collar, is a tender, flavourful fish dish from Japan. It refers to the meat taken from the yellowtail's collar bone area, just below the head. One of my sous-chefs used to make this dish in London. At DOOR73, we opted to give it our own twist with kimchi grilled in olive oil and a ginger-jalapeño dressing.

250 g hamachi kama
60 ml olive oil
150 g kimchi
30 g ginger-jalapeño dressing
6 g salt

Ginger-jalapeño dressing
50 g jalapeños (seeded)
10 g green chilli peppers
100 g fresh ginger, finely chopped
6 g Maldon salt

150 ml grapeseed oil
50 ml light soy sauce
15 ml lemon juice
110 ml rice vinegar

Kimchi
3 Chinese cabbages
500 g salt
4 litres water
90 g ginger, peeled
70 g garlic
350 g white onions
25 g brown sugar
8 ml fish sauce

50 ml light soy sauce
25 g gochujang
30 g salt
100 ml water
25 g corn flour
50 ml sherry vinegar
80 ml rice vinegar
40 g Korean chillies
50 g bonito flakes
2 spring onions, finely chopped
250 g carrots, grated
200 g daikon, grated

METHOD

For the ginger-jalapeño dressing:
Combine all the ingredients and strain through a fine-mesh sieve.

For the kimchi:
Quarter the cabbages and soak them in the salted water for 6 hours. Rinse them and leave them to drain. Combine the ginger with the garlic, white onions, brown sugar, fish sauce, soy sauce, gochujang and salt. Pour the water into a pan and thicken the liquid with corn flour. Add the ginger mixture to the pan. Add the sherry vinegar, rice vinegar, Korean chillies, bonito flakes, spring onions, carrot and daikon and stir until you have a thick paste. Rub the paste into the cabbages and put the cabbages one by one in an airtight jar until the jar is full. Press the cabbage down using your hands until all the excess liquid has escaped from the jar, and then seal the jar with the lid. Store the kimchi somewhere with a constant temperature between 20 and 24 °C. After 3 days, you need to remove the lid daily over the course of 3 weeks; press down the cabbage into the liquid every week (use gloves!) so the cabbage stays nicely submerged under the liquid. The kimchi is ready to be consumed after 3 to 4 weeks.

Grill the fish with enough olive oil, and extra olive oil to the kimchi. Grill for 2 to 3 minutes until everything is sufficiently caramelised. Remove the fish from heat and stick the collar on a skewer. Drizzle the ginger-jalapeño dressing on a plate, serve the hamachi kama on top followed by the kimchi. Finish with the leftover kimchi juice from the airtight container and a splash of olive oil.

MACKEREL WITH SAMBAL AND SOY DRESSING

Preparation time: 45 minutes   Serves 4

This unique combination of mackerel and sambal is one of Syrco Bakker's creations. Sambal is a spicy chilli sauce or paste frequently used in Indonesian cuisine — which also happen to be where Syrco's roots lie. Sambal gives a flavourful kick to the mackerel, which by definition has a fatty texture. The result is a fantastically balanced flavour palette.

1 mackerel (400 to 600 grams)
100 g sambal
50 ml soy dressing
30 g spring onions
30 g glasswort
3 g Maldon salt
1 lemon
20 ml maize oil

Sambal
5 white onions
5 red onions
25 g ginger
80 g lemongrass
7 g coriander seeds
25 g red chilli peppers
3 g lime leaf
30 g garlic
200 ml maize oil
300 g tomato paste

Soy dressing
25 ml soy sauce (Kikkoman)
25 ml sushi vinegar
10 g shiso leaf
10 g shallots, finely chopped
20 ml olive oil

METHOD

For the sambal:
Preheat the oven to 160 °C. Peel and finely chop the onions. Put the onions in baking dish and cover with a lid or another dish. Place the dish in the oven and bake the onions for 25 minutes. Chop the ginger and lemongrass into very fine pieces. Grind the coriander seeds down to a fine powder. Mix all the spices, the finely chopped ginger and lemon grass and maize oil to a fine puree. Put a pan over heat and add the spiced puree; sauté for 5 minutes. Add the chopped onions, stir well and cook for 20 minutes. Stir regularly. After 20 minutes, add the tomato paste and leave the mixture to simmer for 3 1/2 hours. Allow the sambal to cool before use.

For the soy dressing:
Combine all the ingredients and let the dressing steep for 3 hours. Strain the liquid through a sieve and add a little bit of extra olive oil just before serving.

First, fillet the fish, season with salt and bake the fish skin-side down in parchment paper with maize oil over low heat. Arrange the mackerel on a plate and spoon a dollop of sambal on top. Garnish with the soy dressing, spring onion and glasswort. Season with a pinch of Maldon salt and lemon zest.

HANNES' SOFT TOUCH

E A significant milestone in DOOR73's evolution was the arrival of Hannes Verniers. Given that I often hear that I generally come across as rugged and raw, I knew that the front of house at DOOR73 needed a certain softness to achieve the optimal balance in our restaurant. Every day, I continue to be amazed at the insight into human nature that Hannes brings to the table at every service. He knows how to run a professional service while always maintaining that personal connection. Hannes is keen, intelligent, and opinionated, although he's man enough to admit when he's at fault. And he's someone who takes matters into his own hands. A perfect example is our drinks menu, which he felt didn't complement the food I served enough. Drawing on his expertise regarding beverages, he started to create his own cocktails and mocktails, and even a liqueur as a digestif. Hannes also encourages me to make my own choices in terms of wines. Marcelo is more the type that tends towards delicate and subtle wines, while I tend to choose bold wines that pack a punch. That is why I am immensely proud that we can work with small-scale local Greek vineyards. During my next visits to Crete, I plan to visit more vineyards.

From clashing personalities to friendship

H The catering industry took centre stage in my life from an early age. When I was 17 years old, I got a job working weekends at a restaurant. Although I later went on to study History and even briefly ended up working in the education sector, I couldn't leave the restaurant world behind me. Interacting with guests is one particular aspect that draws me to the field.

After years of working in different types of businesses, such as Simon Says and Martino, I wanted to find a job with greater depth. OAK was my favourite restaurant, so I decided to take the plunge. Marcelo led me to Eric, and the rest is history. Although I was new to the fine-dining segment, I instantly won Eric and Marcelo over with my relaxed style. Eric in particular had a more casual service in mind for DOOR73.

As I'm not averse to change, I gladly took on the challenge. What I particularly missed in my previous jobs was being able to make time for guests. Guests come to a fine-dining restaurant to just let go. That moment when you can gain their confidence by catering to their every need is magical. Though I must admit, this wasn't a conscious shift. My relationship with Eric was full of contrasts. He ran his kitchen like a strict manager, while my approach was more casual. Eric organised his restaurant from his perspective as a chef, while I viewed the restaurant from perspective of the guests' experience. We've made major progress in meeting each other halfway since we started out. Eric has learned to let go, and I have gained a wealth of knowledge from his kitchen and product expertise. To this day, clashes still aren't a problem. Pleasing each other gets us nowhere.

In our line of work, you need experience and openness when dealing with various situations. Especially at Martino, I discovered that a restaurant is a place where you meet countless different types of people: visitors, locals, nightlife enthusiasts, families, celebrities... Putting yourself forward is no use; you must be humble when working in the hospitality sector. I am absolutely not the type that hides behind titles. Scrubbing toilets is not beneath me and narrow-mindedness is toxic.

The blurring of boundaries between the kitchen and service has become firmly embedded in DOOR73's DNA. I taste the new dishes and share my findings with Eric. But it also happens that I have Eric try one of my cocktails, which in turn inspires him to think up a dish. When Eric decided to take his langoustines with shiso and lime off the menu, I took that flavour combination and developed a new cocktail. Or another example: when I was in Athens, I visited a Tiki cocktail bar on Eric's recommendation. That's where I tasted a cocktail with a blend of five different rums, which inspired me to develop my own blend for DOOR73 as a basis for our Dark & Stormy.

And sometimes, it's just a matter of serendipity. One day, when one of our candles caught fire, and I succeeded in putting the fire out in a cloud of smoke, my reaction towards our guests was: 'We don't only smoke things in the kitchen.' And that led to the Smoked Negroni.

It's hard to pinpoint my inspiration to a single source. I'm too eclectic for that.

In general, our cocktails are a reflection of our food: comforting and bursting with flavour. I love layering and adding taste variation for increased intensity, which is essential to a restaurant's cocktail menu. Our drinks, like the smoked negroni or our whisky sour, need to intrigue and hold their own next to a dish.

A refined sharing concept with personalised service

Today we have a far more extensive drinks menu than most fine-dining restaurants. I have spent many hours developing a menu where everyone can find something they like. Whether you drink alcohol or not, whether prefer something salty, bitter, or hearty; you'll find it on our menu. That's also the case with our wine menu, which is built up from fresh to juicy to funky or strong. It contains both organic wines as well as the more classic vinification techniques, not to mention our Greek wines. Greek wines are highly suitable for our cuisine, in particular given Eric's roots and taste profile. I greatly admire his cooking style with simple yet cosmopolitan and distinctive flavours. A dish such as ray with gremolata and jalapeño is both familiar and surprising in equal measure. These unorthodox dishes are what give DOOR73 its strong identity.

Eric and I hate it when DOOR73 is referred to as a shared-dining concept. The sharing part refers to the atmosphere and our philosophy. We try to relate our story through the flavours, the atmosphere and our focus on drinks.

Both Eric and I are still brimming with enthusiasm and creativity. The future of DOOR73 will be marked by a continued focus on refinement and detail, both in terms of dishes and the dining experience. I'm already looking forward to it. And I now feel that Eric, Marcelo, and Dominik have come to appreciate me. Calling someone out or humiliating someone doesn't happen here. Everyone can be themselves, and that makes room for spontaneous creativity. I personally feel that I am encouraged to grow. Much of this growth has to do with the solid foundation that Dominik established at the beginning. He provides a sense of calm. And that segues back to my domain: calmness, structure, and excellent service tailored to each guest.

DESSERTS

LEMON KATAIFI WITH RAS-EL-HANOUT AND BUTTERMILK ICE CREAM

Preparation time: 3 to 4 hours   Serves 2-4

Kataifi is a delightfully sweet pastry made with fine strands of dough; some people compare it to baklava, although the dough is completely different. In the traditional version, the sweet flavours dominate. I wanted to think up a more balanced dessert for the restaurant. So I came up with a Greek-style lemon cake, enriched with herbs from the Middle East.

20 g butter
60 g kataifi
100 g lemon pastry cream
30 g pistachios
30 g lemon jelly
10 g ras-el-hanout
120 ml buttermilk ice cream

Buttermilk ice cream
150 ml milk
950 ml buttermilk
350 g full-fat whipping cream (40%)
125 g sugar
90 g glucose

Lemon pastry cream
50 g lemon curd
100 g pastry cream
20 g lemon jelly
50 g full-fat cream

Pastry cream
7 g gelatine
460 ml milk
90 g sugar
90 g egg yolk
28 g corn flour
55 g butter

Lemon curd
100 g white chocolate
25 g cocoa butter
4 g lemon peel
30 g sugar
140 g egg yolk
120 ml lemon juice

Lemon jelly
250 ml lemon juice
125 g sugar
125 ml water
6 g agar

METHOD

Preheat the oven to 180 °C.
Melt the butter and coat half the kataifi with the butter.
Slide the kataifi in a metal wrap with a diameter of 3 cm and bake in the oven for 12 to 14 minutes until golden brown.

For the buttermilk ice cream:
Combine all the ingredients in a bowl and use the ice cream machine to churn into an ice cream.

For the pastry cream:
Soak the gelatine in iced water until soft.
Heat the milk in a saucepan until it reaches a temperature of 80 °C.
In a bowl, combine the sugar, egg yolk and corn flour and beat for 1 to 2 minutes to a foamy mixture.
Slowly add the milk and mix thoroughly.
Transfer the mixture to the pan over low heat and stir constantly until the cream thickens.
Remove the pan from heat and add the gelatine together with the butter.
Blend to form an emulsion and leave in the refrigerator to cool.
Before serving, transfer everything to a bowl and beat the mixture until smooth and creamy.

For the lemon curd:
Add the white chocolate and cocoa butter to a deep bowl.
In a saucepan, heat the lemon peel, sugar, egg yolk and lemon juice over low heat. Stir with a whisk until the mixture thickens. Spoon the mixture into the bowl with the white chocolate and the cocoa butter and combine to create a smooth paste.
Strain the curd through a sieve to remove any eggy lumps from the curd.
Leave the lemon curd in the refrigerator for 3 to 4 hours to allow it to firm up.

For the lemon jelly:
Put all the ingredients in a pan and heat to 90 °C.
Spread the jelly out on a tray and put it in the refrigerator.
Transfer the cool, firm jelly to a bowl and mix into a creamy gel.

For the lemon pastry cream:
Combine the lemon curd and the pastry cream with the lemon jelly.
Beat the whipping cream until fluffy and combine with the full cream.

Grind the pistachios down to a powder.
Fill the kataifi with the lemon pastry cream and coat both sides with the pistachio powder.
Place the stuffed kataifi on a plate and add the lemon jelly.
Garnish with a pinch of pistachio powder, ras-el-hanout on top and serve a scoop of buttermilk ice cream on the side.

RASPBERRY SUNDAE WITH YUZU AND YOGHURT

Preparation time: 2 hours Serves 2

The first time I served this dessert — a unique combination of raspberry and yuzu — was at Tomorrowland. And it proved to be such a success that I decided to serve this dessert to our guests at DOOR73. A brilliant move!

30 g raspberry mousse
20 g vanilla cake
80 ml vanilla ice cream
40 g yoghurt foam
10 g yuzu jelly
30 ml vanilla sauce
30 ml raspberry-yuzu dressing
2 raspberries

Raspberry mousse
14 g gelatine
250 ml milk
3 vanilla beans
475 g white chocolate
500 g full-fat whipping cream (40% fat)
200 g raspberry puree

Vanilla cake
170 g butter
250 g sugar
5 g salt
1 vanilla bean
3 eggs
280 g flour
240 ml buttermilk
10 g baking powder

Vanilla ice cream
1 litre milk
250 g full-fat whipping cream (40% fat)
120 g sugar
80 g glucose
3 vanilla beans

Yoghurt foam
1500 g yoghurt
800 ml milk
12 g Sucro Emul (emulsifier)
40 g pro espuma
220 g confectioner's sugar
7 g citric acid

Yuzu jelly
500 g yuzu
250 g sugar
250 ml water
10 g agar

Vanilla sauce
250 g whipping cream
950 ml milk
160 g sugar
1 vanilla bean
135 g egg yolk

Raspberry-yuzu dressing
50 g confectioner's sugar
180 g raspberry puree
5 ml yuzu juice
220 g frozen raspberries

METHOD

For the raspberry mousse:
First, soak the gelatine.
Heat the milk and add the vanilla together with the gelatine.
Let everything melt and then heat the mixture to 80 °C.
Add the white chocolate and blend with the stick blender.
Whip the cream until fluffy and fold into the chocolate mixture.
Combine with the raspberry puree and then leave the mousse to set for at least 4 hours in the refrigerator.

For the vanilla cake:
Preheat the oven to 175 °C.
Beat the butter with the sugar, salt and vanilla. Slowly add the eggs to the mixture.
Then add half the flour, continue with the buttermilk, and finish with the remaining flour and the baking powder.
Bake the cake in the oven for 20 to 25 minutes.
Slice the cake in small rings measuring 3 centimetres.

For the vanilla ice cream:
Combine all the ingredients in a bowl and use the ice cream machine to churn into an ice cream.

For the yoghurt foam:
Combine all the ingredients in a bowl and put the foam into a siphon; shake well before use.

For the yuzu jelly:
Combine all the ingredients and heat them to 90 °C.
Spoon the mixture into a tray, leave it to cool in the refrigerator and combine later to form the jelly.

For the vanilla sauce:
Combine all the ingredients in a small pan.
Slowly bring the mixture to a boil, stirring constantly.
Remove the pan from heat once the sauce has the desired consistency (usually at a temperature of around 82 °C).
Let the sauce rest for 1 hour at room temperature.
Store the sauce for at a little over an hour in the refrigerator before serving.

For the raspberry-yuzu dressing:
Add all the ingredients (except for the yuzu juice) to a medium-sized pan.
Cook for 3 minutes until the sugar has dissolved.
Then add the yuzu juice and keep the dressing in the refrigerator until it is ready to be used.

Start by placing a spoonful of raspberry mousse onto a plate.
Place the vanilla cake on top, add the vanilla ice cream and the yoghurt foam and garnish with two raspberries.
Finish with the yuzu jelly, vanilla sauce and raspberry-yuzu dressing.

CRÈME BRÛLÉE WITH RUM AND BRIOCHE

Preparation time: 4 hours   Serves 2-4

Crème brûlée is a fantastic dessert that has stood the test of time. And yet I wanted to raise this classic dessert to a higher level. My weapons of choice: brioche and rum. The resulting combination of flavours and textures provides a mouth-watering contrast.

160 g crème brûlée
120 ml vanilla sauce
80 g white chocolate feuilletine
100 g brioche bread

Crème brûlée
870 g full-fat whipping cream (40%)
2 vanilla beans
165 g sugar
165 g egg yolk
165 g egg
85 ml rum

Vanilla sauce
475 g full-fat whipping cream (40%)
125 ml milk
80 g sugar
70 g egg yolk
1 vanilla bean

White chocolate feuilletine
125 g white chocolate
90 g cocoa butter
75 g feuilletine
100 g crispy rice
5 g Maldon salt
50 g white chocolate pearls

Brioche
4 eggs
100 ml milk
500 g T65 flour (+ extra for flouring the workbench)
10 g salt
20 g yeast
60 g granulated sugar
20 g butter
1 egg yolk
20 ml water

METHOD

For the crème brûlée:
Preheat the oven to 90 °C.
Heat the whipping cream, the vanilla, and half of the sugar in a saucepan until the sugar has melted. Check to see whether the hot cream has reached a temperature of 80 °C.
Combine the egg yolk, the eggs and the remaining sugar in a bowl. Slowly pour in the hot cream and combine.
Then add the rum, mix thoroughly and pour the mixture into crème brûlée moulds.
Place the moulds in the oven for 43 to 48 minutes until the crème brûlée feels firm.
Remove from the oven and store them in the freezer for 2 hours.
After defrosting, coat the crème brûlée with a bit of extra sugar, and caramelise the sugar à la minute just before serving.

For the vanilla sauce:
Combine all the ingredients in a small pan.
Slowly bring the mixture to a boil, stirring constantly.
Remove the pan from heat once the sauce has the desired consistency (usually at a temperature of around 82 °C).
Let the sauce rest for 1 hour at room temperature.
Store the sauce for at a little over an hour in the refrigerator before serving.

For the feuilletine:
Melt the chocolate au bain marie with the cocoa butter.
Remove from heat and let the mixture cool to about 40 °C.
Add the remaining ingredients and stir well.
Press the feuilletine into cooking rings and place in the fridge until use.

For the brioche:
Use a hand mixer with a dough hook attachment. Combine the eggs with the milk in a bowl at the lowest speed setting.
Add the flour, the salt and the yeast. Mix for another 2 minutes to combine the ingredients into a homogenous whole.
Stop mixing and scrape the sides of the bowl. Increase the speed setting on your mixer and mix for another 2 minutes.
With the mixer turning at high speed, slowly and gradually stir in the granulated

sugar. Make sure the sugar has dissolved before adding more — the entire process should take up about 5 minutes. As the sugar is incorporated in the dough, it will come away from the sides of the bowl.
Add all the butter. Mix for a further 10 minutes at high speed until the butter is fully incorporated. Scrape the bowl clean at least once during this process. The dough will start to lump around the hook and will come away from the sides of the bowl with a slight beating sound. Check to see if the dough is shiny, smooth and moist. If it is, then your dough is ready.

Grease a large bowl with cooking spray.
Roll the dough around in the bowl so it is completely coated with the spray.
Cover the bowl with cling film. Leave the dough in a warm spot (between 25 and 30 °C) for one hour.
Coat your workbench with a thin layer of flour, remove the dough from the bowl and place it on your work surface.
Carefully fold the dough into three parts, like folding a letter.
Turn the dough 90° and fold again in the same way.
Then return the dough to the bowl, cover the bowl and leave the dough to prove for another 30 minutes.
Store the dough in the refrigerator for 12 hours.
Roll out into 80-gram pieces.
Place the pieces in small baking tins, brush a layer of lightly beaten egg yolk (mixed with water) over the top and allow the mini brioches to prove for 30-40 minutes.
Bake the brioche for 12 minutes in an oven preheated to 180 °C and leave to cool before serving.
Slice the brioche into thick 5-centimetre slices and then in rings 7 centimetres in diameter.
Drizzle 2 spoonfuls vanilla sauce and 5 ml rum over each brioche.
Return the brioche to the oven for another 2-3 minutes at 200 °C so the brioche can absorb the cream and caramelise.

Top the feuilletine with the crème brûlée and caramelise the sugar with a kitchen torch.
Then arrange the feuilletine on top of the brioche, garnish with the vanilla sauce and serve.

DONUTS WITH VANILLA ICE CREAM AND PISTACHIO HALVA

Preparation time: 18 hours   Serves 6-8

All my life, I have been passionate about donuts and other sweet treats. But like so many of us, I didn't really start to do any serious baking until the COVID-19 pandemic. I took a donut recipe from a cookbook from chef Thomas Keller as my starting point. I added an exotic twist with the pistachio halva, a typically Middle Eastern ingredient that should preferably be kept in the freezer.

500 g T65 flour (+ extra for flouring the workbench)
20 g yeast
375 g sugar
9 g salt
210 ml milk
9 g vanilla extract
50 g butter
1 litre oil for deep frying
1 vanilla bean
100 g pistachio halva
100 ml vanilla ice cream
20 g butterscotch caramel
30 g lemon verbena pastry cream

Vanilla ice cream
1 litre milk
250 g full-fat whipping cream (40% fat)
120 g sugar
80 g glucose
3 vanilla beans

Butterscotch caramel
250 g sugar
30 ml water
25 g butter
200 g full-fat whipping cream (40% fat)

Lemon verbena pastry cream
460 ml milk
20 g lemon verbena
1 vanilla bean
100 g sugar
5 egg yolks
25 g corn flour
2 g gelatine
55 g unsalted butter

METHOD

For the donuts:
Dust your work surface with flour and grease a large bowl with cooking spray.
Add the flour and yeast to a mixing bowl and mix for 15 seconds so the yeast is incorporate evenly into the flour.
Add 75 g sugar, salt, milk and vanilla extract and mix at a low speed setting for 4 minutes.
Continue to mix at low speed for 30 minutes; bits of dough will still stick to the side of the bowl afterwards.
Add the butter in separate portions and make sure the butter is well incorporated before adding the next portion.
Scrape the sides and the bottom of the bowl and remove any leftover dough from the dough hook.
Mix for an additional 5 minutes.
Use a scraper to remove the dough from the sides and bottom of the bowl and roll the dough out on your work surface — only add flour if needed to prevent the dough from sticking to your workbench.
Carefully pat the dough with your hands into a rectangular shape; the dough will feel sticky.
Stretch the left side of the dough out and fold it over two-thirds of the dough. Stretch it out once again on the right-hand side and fold it over to the left, as if folding a letter. Repeat this process from top to bottom and vice versa.
Turn the dough over, pick it up with a scraper and place it seam-side down in the prepared bowl.
Cover the bowl with cling film or a clean kitchen towel and leave for 1 hour at room temperature.
Use the scraper to loosen the dough from the sides and roll the dough out on a work surface (lightly) dusted with flour.
Carefully but firmly pat the dough into a rectangle and press any large air bubbles out to the sides and out of the dough.
Repeat the stretch-and-fold process once more and place the dough seam-side down in the bowl a second time.
Cover and leave overnight in the refrigerator.

Roll the dough out on a work surface dusted with flour, turn it over and place the dough on parchment paper.
Let the dough cool in the refrigerator for 30 minutes or place it in the freezer for 10 minutes until the dough is firm enough to cut.
Line a baking tray with parchment paper and lightly coat the parchment paper with cooking spray.

Cut (with the 8-centimetre blade from your mixer) eight circles from the dough and then cut holes in the middle (with the 4-centimetre blade from your mixer).
Brush off any excess flour and place the dough on the lined baking tray. Throw away the holes after proving or baking.
Cover the baking tray with cling film and allow the dough to prove for 2 to 3 hours until they have doubled in size. Lightly press the donut with your finger to see if your fingerprint leaves a dent in the dough. If it does, the dough is ready.

Start cooking the donuts.

Pour a layer of oil 3 centimetres deep in a cast-iron pan; make sure the oil is deep enough that the donuts can float freely and that any oil spatters reach no further than the bottom two thirds of the pan. Preheat the oil to 170 °C.

Place a wire cooling rack on a baking tray.

Add 300 g sugar to a large bowl. Scrape the vanilla bean.

Add the vanilla bean scrapings to the sugar and stir with your hands to make vanilla sugar.

Carefully drop four donuts into the oil and fry them for 30 seconds. Are they not firm enough yet? Increase the temperature.

Turn the donuts over and fry them for 45 seconds on one side. Turn them over again and fry them for another 45 seconds on the other side until golden brown.

Place the donuts on the cooling rack and leave them to cool as you fry the second batch.

Just before placing the second donut on the rack, roll the first donut through the vanilla sugar.

Let the second batch cool before rolling them through the vanilla sugar.

Ideally, you should eat the donuts when they're freshly fried, but you can keep them up to 1 day in an airtight container.

For the butterscotch caramel:
Add the sugar and water to a small saucepan.
Cook slowly to a caramel, add the butter and stir briefly.
Remove the mixture from the heat, add the cream and stir.
Let the caramel cool before use.

For the lemon verbena pastry cream:
Heat the milk to 80 °C and infuse with the fresh lemon verbena for 1 hour.
Strain the infused milk through a sieve and set aside.
Put the milk together with the vanilla in a saucepan and bring to a boil.
Combine the sugar and egg yolks with the corn flour in a separate bowl.
Slowly add the milk to the sugar mixture and then transfer everything back to the saucepan.
Stir over low heat until the cream thickens.
Soften the gelatine by soaking it in iced water.
Remove the pan from heat and add the gelatine together with the butter.

For the vanilla ice cream:
Combine all the ingredients in a bowl and use the ice cream machine to churn into an ice cream.

Spoon a spoonful of lemon verbena pastry cream in the middle of the donut, followed by the ice cream and finally the butterscotch caramel.

Garnish by grating the frozen pistachio halva over the donuts.

APPLE PIE WITH MASTIHA ICE CREAM

Preparation time: 5 hours   Serves 4-6

Mastiha is a resin from the mastic tree that grows on the Greek island of Chios. This resin is often used in Mediterranean and Arabian desserts such as cake and pudding, but also in sweets and for flavouring coffee and tea. When combined with sugar, as we have done in this recipe for mastiha ice cream, mastiha adds an immense depth of flavour to this classic apple pie.

250 g flour
30 g ground almonds
120 g unsalted butter
100 g confectioner's sugar
1 egg
100 g apple compote
3 caramelised apple rings
120 ml mastiha ice cream

Apple compote
6 Granny Smith apples
1 vanilla bean
100 g sugar
280 ml sparkling white wine

Caramelised apple rings
3 Granny Smith apples
120 g caramel powder

Mastiha ice cream
1 litre milk
30 g mastiha powder
250 g full-fat cream
100 g sugar
80 g glucose

METHOD

Start by making the sweet tart dough.
Sieve the flour and the ground almonds into a large bowl and set aside.
Combine the butter and the sugar in a mixer bowl with a spatula. Add the egg and beat into a homogenous whole.
Add the dry ingredients in one go and continue to mix at low speed until the dough comes together. (Don't mix the dough any longer than this, otherwise it will become hard to roll out).
Remove the dough from the bowl and form into a disc.
Wrap the dough in plastic film and store it in the refrigerator for at least 20 minutes. If you wish to use the dough after two days, we recommend storing it in the freezer so the dough doesn't oxidate or turn grey. Please note: If you freeze the dough, leave it to defrost overnight before rolling it out.
Roll out the dough and cut it into 4-centimetre circles. Place the dough in the moulds.
Slice the remaining dough into 2-centimetre strips and spread it out nicely round the sides of the mould.
Let the dough firm up in the refrigerator for 1 hour before baking the pastries until golden brown for 10 to 15 minutes in an oven preheated to 170 °C.

For the apple compote:
Peel and core the apples and chop into small pieces.
Put them together with the remaining ingredients in a pan and cover with parchment paper.
Cook over low heat to a compote.
Combine all the ingredients in a blender and mix.

For the caramelised apple rings:
Slice the apples using a mandolin into long strips and roll them into a ring.
Put them on a baking tray lined with foil, add the caramel powder and cover with another layer of foil.
Place the apple rings for 15 to 20 minutes in the oven at 140 °C.
Leave to cool in the refrigerator before use.

For the mastiha ice cream:
Combine all the ingredients in a bowl and use the ice cream machine to churn into an ice cream.

Compose your dessert plate by starting with the sweet tart pastry, add the apple compote followed by the caramelised apple rings, and finish with a scoop of mastiha ice cream.

ERIC IVANIDIS

No one knows that you...
Love to paint. My father used to paint and encouraged me to take up the brush at an early age. I compare it a little to Marcelo's passion for playing the guitar. If he hadn't become a chef, he would definitely have been a musician.

What is your favourite aperitif?
Negroni, a drink that I recently discovered in Belgium. However, my Greek blood ensures that I tend to get quite loud after a couple of sips. Marcelo is more of a whisky-sour man.

You can't live without...
Music. The first thing I do when I get up in the morning is put on a record. It's something I share with my daughter. She then immediately starts to sing along and dance.

What is your personal definition of luxury?
I don't care much for material wealth. For me, luxury means engaging in new experiences and being able to make the time for them. Travelling, spending time with my daughter, going to the beach with my friends. Those kinds of things.

What is the first thing you do after service has finished?
I first place my orders, and then I review the day with my team over drinks.

What about Marcelo are you envious of?
I think he's incredibly organised. And Marcelo is the type that always thinks about the future and makes decisions with that in mind. I tend to live more in the moment. I usually need a healthy dose of stress before I spring into action.

MARCELO BALLARDIN

At the weekend, you most like to eat…
Whatever Dominik makes for us. He makes a fantastic pasta al ragù.

What do you appreciate the most about Eric?
His honesty. He will always tell you the truth without beating around the bush. Pretending or lying is unnatural for him. His candour makes him a true friend.

Which chefs do you admire?
There are several, especially the ones I've worked for, such as Heston Blumenthal, Sergio Herman, and Rasmus Kofoed. I have warm memories of my time with Yotam Ottolenghi in particular. His influence is unprecedented; he has spent 15 years building his empire into what it is today. His test kitchen is impressive. He develops every recipe and every concept in his own creative universe. He plants his seeds there as it were, and his staff nurtures those seeds to help them grow and flourish. I feel truly inspired when I'm there.

What do you dream about nowadays?
Starting a restaurant in L.A. I don't know if Eric and I will ever end up working in the same kitchen again, but I can see us developing a new concept together.

What is the biggest difference between the kitchens of OAK and DOOR73?
Form and experience. Eric cooks à la carte, and I apply myself to creating a gastronomic experience by serving prepared menus. His cuisine is relatively recognisable: if you order langoustines at DOOR73, you will be served gorgeously grilled langoustines, while I serve the same langoustine at OAK in three different ways and in greater detail.

What would you like to change about OAK in the long term?
I would like to focus more on the harvesting and supply of my products and cook à la minute. That I, as a chef, would let our guests know that we have sea bass or turbot available and then ask them how they would like to have it served: grilled or poached. That's how you return to the essence of cooking. The older I get, the more to the point I would like to cook.

DOOR73 would never have existed without the invaluable efforts of a select number of people. I want to give my heartfelt thanks to Melissa Breuk, our first maître d'hôtel at the restaurant. The way in which she devoted her heart and soul to her role will remain with me for years to come. Thank you also to Lode Avet for designing our distinctive logo, still one of the best in existence. Merita Fakira, for the faultless structure she adopted for our reservations system. Njegoš Kaličanin is a good friend of Eric's and mine and a talented colleague we could always call on. Eleni Tsiamati, who is always prepared to help out with service or washing dishes: you are essential to our team. I am also thankful for chef Theocharis Viglakis, who helped Eric develop his own path. Thank you to Lizette Viaene, for her unique personality and mindset and because she chose us when we needed someone like her the most.
And let's not forget Hannes Verniers, whose sharp tongue and flair drove our service team to new heights. Hannes is synonymous with DOOR73. He and Eric intuitively inspire each other to bring out the very best in themselves every day – and to surpass themselves the next day.

Eric, I am delighted to have been a privileged witness to your development as a loving father and the exceptionally creative chef you are today. In fact, I believe you have so much more hidden talent just waiting to be explored. I look forward to seeing more of that talent in the near future. Dear friend, thank you for everything. I wish you nothing but the brightest future.

And thank you to Dominik. He is a tower of strength in my world, the one person who manages to bring order and structure into our lives and does so with flair. He is a visionary who not only believed in me but also shares and carries forward Eric's culinary vision. Dominik, I will always be thankful to you, and give you all my love to the moon and back.

Marcelo

Publishing a book is not something you do alone; it's a team effort. Not only am I thankful to our loyal partners and guests at the restaurant, but when developing my recipes, I have also been inspired by countless chefs, restaurants, and staff that have been part of my world. Thanks to all of you, I keep finding the drive to create and undertake new projects. Thank you!

I would also like to thank several people in particular:

- My parents for letting me experience the luxury of delicious food.
- My teacher, Fanis Stathis from Athens, who spontaneously became my mentor.
- Our suppliers and guests who ensure that we can carry out our job with passion every day.
- Our fantastic team, led by Hannes Verviers, the driving force behind DOOR73.
- Lannoo Publishers for believing in me before the book. Thank you also to the designers at KaaTigo, photographer Kris Vlegels and author Femke Vandevelde.
- Dominik, to whom I can always turn for solid advice.
- Marcelo, my mentor, brother, best friend and business partner, for the many years we spent together.
- My wife Eleni for her support through thick and thin and for helping me turn all my dreams into reality.
- My daughter Athina for her cheerful, sunny disposition and bursts of laughter.

Eric

I got to know Eric when he started on Marcelo's team at Pure C. They have come a long way together since then, first as colleagues under chef Syrco Bakker, and later as chef and sous chef at OAK. Today, Marcelo and Eric each stand at the helm of their own restaurant. In my eyes, it was a journey that took its natural course. Eric and Marcelo are where they are today because of their learning experiences at Pure C and their strong characters. Together, we form a close family. I see it as a huge privilege that I can try out the new menu at OAK with my mother and, at the same time, experience a fantastic evening with my partner at DOOR73. I will never take either of these experiences for granted.

Having been an entrepreneur for some time and having instantly noticed Marcelo and Eric's drive as a team, it didn't take long before I challenged them to work on their own project. Behind the scenes, I worked on creating an administrative backbone so they could explore their creativity to their heart's content. To this day, their mutual playing on each other's strengths continues to be a recipe for success.

Given that Eric has helped shape Marcelo's dream, Marcelo and I felt it was important that we reciprocate that support by assisting Eric to fulfil his dream. There was no way that he could develop further and become a chef at OAK. Moreover, he yearned for his own project to work on. Precisely on the day that Eric told Marcelo that his story at OAK would end for that very reason, I heard that a perfect restaurant location had been put up for sale just 100 meters down the road – as if it was meant to be. It was an opportunity I had to take. DOOR73's first years are behind us today, and Eric is more ready than ever to show what he is capable of.

Before the first words of Marcelo's first book were ever put onto paper, the idea for a second book was already taking shape. That's how intertwined the two worlds that make up OAK and DOOR73 are. And that Marcelo and Eric's stories are far from finished will undoubtedly become apparent in the future.

To all our guests at OAK and DOOR73: Here's to many more years together.

See you soon,
Dominik

INGREDIENT INDEX

A
Agar	168, 172
Aji Amarillo	90
Allspice	82
Amaretto	28
Amaro	28
Anchovies	126
Angostura bitters	22
Apple (Granny Smith)	184
Aquafaba	22
Artichoke	76
Asparagus (green)	116
Aubergine	82, 92
Avocado	60

B
Bacon	44, 96
Baharat spices	153
Baking powder	172
Basil	92
Basil (Thai)	78
Bay leaf	82, 86
Beetroot	40, 44
Bell pepper (green)	153
Bell pepper (red)	100, 142
Blueberry	44
Bonitoflakes	158
Bread (brioche)	176
Bread (sourdough)	64, 116
Brioche	44
Buckwheat	116
Burrata	112
Butter beans	118
Buttermilk	168, 172

C
Cachaça	26
Calamari	114
Calvados	44
Cane sugar	26
Cape gooseberry	60
Caper	54, 126
Caper leaves	64
Caramel powder	184
Cardamom	30
Carrot	86, 100, 153, 158
Cashew	148
Cauliflower	122
Cayenne pepper	58, 90, 148, 153
Celery	146, 154
Celery seed	58, 90, 148
Cherry liqueur	28
Cherry tomato	92, 112
Chicken liver	44
Chicken seasoning	90
Chicken skin	90
Chicken wings	58
Chilli	96, 118, 128, 136, 138, 142, 148, 153, 158, 160
Chilli flakes (red)	116, 153
Chilli powder	112
Chinese cabbage	158

Chives 62, 112, 138
Chocolate (white)	168, 172, 176
Chocolate pearls (white)	176
Cider (apple)	58
Cinnamon stick	82, 100, 144
Citric acid	172
Clams	78
Clams	60
Cloves	153
Cocoa butter	168, 176
Coconut milk	128, 142
Cod	114, 128
Cod roe	62, 70, 94
Cognac	30, 86
Coriander	60, 114, 122, 128, 142, 148, 153
Coriander powder	138
Coriander seeds	30, 86, 118, 122, 136, 153, 160
Corn flour	158, 168, 180
Corn-fed chicken breasts	138
Crab (North Sea)	154
Crab (soft-shell)	66
Crab claws	154
Crayfish claws	154
Cream	168, 176, 184
Cretan raki	50
Cucumber	66, 144, 146
Cumin	58, 90, 112, 148
Cumin powder	136, 138
Cumin seeds	122, 136
Curry paste (red)	118, 128, 148
Curry powder	96, 128

D
Daikon	66, 144, 158
Date tomatoes (dried)	64
Dill	114
Dried tomato powder	112
Dried tomato powder	82, 96
Duck legs	144

E
Ears of fresh sweetcorn	52
Egg	30, 44, 50, 54, 58, 66, 82, 94, 96, 114, 154, 168, 172, 176, 180, 184
Emmental cheese	82
Essential oil (lemongrass)	26

F
Fennel fronds	126
Feta	40, 64, 100, 146
Feuilletine	176
Fish sauce	128, 158
Flour	66, 82, 94, 114, 172, 184
Flour (corn)	50
Flour (T00)	54
Flour (T55)	50
Flour (T65)	44, 176, 180
Flour (tapioca)	90
Flour (tempura)	66
Full-fat whipping cream	168, 172, 176, 180

G
Gambero rosso	142
Garam masala	138
Garlic	40, 60, 64, 78, 82, 86, 90, 92, 94, 96, 102, 112, 116, 118, 122, 128, 136, 138, 142, 153, 158, 160
Garlic (confit)	58
Garlic powder	58, 82, 90, 114, 148
Gelatine	168, 172, 180
Ginger	118, 128, 138, 158, 160
Ginger beer	24, 26
Glasswort	160
Glucose	168, 172, 180, 184
Gochujang	158
Gouda	50
Grape leaves (salted)	70
Grappa	50
Greek pasta	100
Greek yoghurt	40, 60, 122, 136, 138
Ground almonds	184
Gurnard (red)	94

H
Hamachi kama	158
Hazelnut	122
Holstein beef (smoked)	54

I
Iced water	66

J
Jalapeño	153, 158
Juice (apple)	24, 146
Juice (blueberry)	24
Juice (cherry)	28
Juice (lime)	128
Juice (pineapple)	30
Juice (yuzu)	118, 172

K
Kaffir lime leaves	128
Kataifi	138, 168
Kefalotyri	100
Ketchup	148, 153
Kritamo	126
Kritharaki	100, 153

L
Lamb shanks	86
Leek	96
Lemon	60, 62, 64, 70, 94, 96, 112, 122, 126, 136, 138, 146, 153, 154, 158, 160, 168
Lemon verbena	180
Lemongrass	118, 128, 160

198

Lemongrass stalks	26	Pepper (Sichuan)	30	Sugar (granulated)	44, 176
Lime	24, 60, 70, 78, 118	Pickles	44, 126	Sumac	62, 70, 94
Lime leaf	118, 160	Pimenta-de-bode chilli	142		

M

Mackerel	160
Madeira	44
Manestra	100
Mango	144
Maple syrup	44
Mastiha powder	184
Milk	30, 44, 54, 82, 100, 114, 168, 172, 176, 180, 184
Mint	50, 122
Miso (brown)	122
Mizithra cheese	50
Mussels	60, 102
Mustard	96, 153
Mustard greens	54
Mustard seeds	40, 54

N

Noilly Prat	154
Nori (sheet)	66
Nutmeg	84

O

Oil (deep frying)	180
Oil (grapeseed)	158
Oil (maize)	54, 58, 60, 62, 64, 66, 70, 76, 94, 112, 118, 126, 136, 138, 142, 146, 154, 160
Oil (palm)	142
Oil (rice bran)	154
Oil (sunflower)	154
Onion (red)	60, 76, 100, 118, 160
Onion (white)	44, 62, 70, 86, 94, 118, 136, 138, 142, 153, 158, 160
Onion (yellow)	116
Onion powder	58, 90, 148
Oregano	40, 64, 82, 146
Ossobuco	100
Oyster sauce	154

P

Pan de cristal	70
Panko	94, 96
Panko dough	70, 94
Parmesan cheese	52, 82, 92, 112, 126, 154
Parsley	86, 92, 94, 112, 114, 122, 126, 154
Parsley (blend)	96
Passata	86
Passion fruit	26
Pastis	28
Pecorino	82, 116
Pepper (green)	122
Pepper (Jamaican)	30
Pepper (kampot)	144
Pepper (maceron)	144
Pepper (red)	112

Pepper (Sichuan)	30
Pickles	44, 126
Pimenta-de-bode chilli	142
Pine nuts	112
Pineapple	30
Pistachio halva	180
Pistachios	112, 168
Ponzu	118
Poppy seed	116
Port (white)	154
Portobello	136
Potato	94, 96
Potato (Maris Piper)	82
Pro espuma	172
Puff pastry	114

Q

Quinoa	66

R

Ramson	76
Ras el Hanout	168
Raspberry	172
Razor clams	60, 102
Rhum	30, 176
Ricard	154
Rice (crispy)	176
Ricotta	50, 64
Rosemary	86

S

Sage	96
Salt (flakes)	136
Salt (Maldon)	44, 54, 70, 116, 158, 160, 176
Sardines	70
Scallops	102
Sea bass	126
Sea bream	60
Sesame seeds	50, 116, 122
Shallots	44, 90, 96, 126, 153, 160
Shiso (leaf)	160
Short ribs	148
Shrimps	114, 154
Smoked paprika powder	58, 148
Sobrasada	154
Sofrito	153
Soy sauce	58, 66, 78, 90, 118, 122, 144, 148, 154, 158, 160
Spring chicken	90
Spring onion	64, 118, 136, 158, 160
Star anise	30, 144, 153
Stracciatella cheese	76
Sucro Emul	172
Sugar	22, 24, 30, 40, 44, 52, 54, 66, 100, 146, 168, 172, 176, 180, 184
Sugar (brown)	58, 90, 118, 128, 138, 144, 148, 158, 172, 184
Sugar (confectioner's)	

T

Tabasco	60, 96, 116, 126, 153
Tahini	122
Thyme	24, 86, 96, 102, 112, 153
Tomato	64, 100, 112, 153
Tomato (canned, chopped)	82
Tomato (Noire d'Antan)	146
Tomato (pulp)	153
Tomato (San Marzano)	116
Tomato paste	82, 86, 90, 100, 118, 136, 138, 148, 153, 160
Tortilla chips	58
Treacle	58, 90, 148
Triple sec	28
Tuna (canned)	54
Tyromalama cheese	50

V

Vanilla bean	22, 24, 172, 176, 180, 184
Vanilla extract	180
Vinegar	44
Vinegar (Cabarnet Sauvignon)	112, 122
Vinegar (Chardonnay)	154
Vinegar (cherry)	153
Vinegar (rice)	158
Vinegar (sherry)	158
Vinegar (sushi)	60, 66, 118, 160
Vinegar (Tosazu dashi)	66
Vinegar (white balsamic)	64, 92
Vinegar (white wine)	90, 112, 136, 138
Vinegar (white)	40, 54

W

Wasabi paste	66
Watercress	144
Whisky	22
Wine (red)	82, 86, 100
Wine (white)	78, 102, 184
Worcestershire sauce	58, 90, 126, 148, 153

Y

Yeast	44, 54, 176, 180
Yoghurt	172
Yuzu	172

CONVERSION TABLE

WEIGHTS FOR DRY INGREDIENTS		OVEN TEMPERATURES		LIQUID MEASURES		
		°C	°F	METRIC	IMPERIAL	US
5 g	1/5 oz	70	155	25 ml	1 fl oz	-
20 g	3/4 oz	80	175	50 ml	2 fl oz	¼ cup
25 g	1 oz	140	275	75 ml	3 fl oz	-
50 g	2 oz	150	300	100 ml	3 ½ fl oz	-
200 g	7 oz	160	325	120 ml	4 fl oz	½ cup
250 g	9 oz	180	350	150 ml	5 fl oz	-
300 g	11 oz	190	375	175 ml	6 fl oz	¾ cup
350 g	12 oz	200	400	200 ml	7 fl oz	-
400 g	14 oz	220	425	250 ml	8 fl oz	1 cup
500 g	1 lb 2 oz			300 ml	10 fl oz/ ½ pint	1¼ cups
550g	1¼ lb			400 ml	14 fl oz	-
600 g	1 lb 5 oz			450 ml	15 fl oz	2 cups/ 1 pint
650 g	1 lb 7 oz			600 ml	1 pint	2½ cups
700 g	1 lb 9 oz			750 ml	1 ¼ pints	-
800 g	1¾ lb			900 ml	1½ pints	-
900 g	2 lb			1 litre	1¾ pints	1 quart
1 kg	2¼ lb					

www.lannoo.com
Register on our web site and we will regularly send you a newsletter with information about new books and interesting, exclusive offers.

Text: Femke Vandevelde
Graphic design: Studio Sissi
Typesetting: Kaatigo
Photography: Kris Vlegels, Meredith Thorina (p. 5)
Translation: Textcase

DOOR73 – Hoogstraat 73, 9000 Gent (BE)
www.door73.be

If you have observations or questions, please contact our editorial office: redactielifestyle@lannoo.com

© Marcelo Ballardin and Eric Ivanidis & Uitgeverij Lannoo nv, Tielt, 2023
D/2023/45/532 – NUR 440
ISBN: 978-94-014-9625-4

All rights reserved. Nothing from this publication may be copied, stored in an automated database and/or be made public in any form or in any way, either electronic, mechanical or in any other manner without the prior written consent of the publisher.